Reinventing
for Competency-Based
Education

Many argue that the conventional high school transcript has become irrelevant to today's best practices in teaching, learning, and assessment. With more and more school leaders turning to alternate, competency-based approaches for learning, crediting and transcripts can follow suit by drawing on badging, micro-crediting, digital portfolios of student work, and other emerging tools. *Reinventing Crediting for Competency-Based Education* explores the need for this transformation while detailing the implementation of promising models, particularly the Mastery Transcript Consortium. Written by an experienced consultant and former school leader, this book will assist school and district administrators in making a forward-thinking crediting and transcript system work for their students' futures.

Jonathan E. Martin is an Arizona based consultant and writer on 21st century learning and assessment. Among his recent affiliations and client organizations are ACT Inc., Mastery Transcript Consortium, EdLeader21, National Association of Independent Schools, Enrollment Management Association, Blackbaud, INDEX, and Think Through Math. From 1996 to 2012 he served as Head of School at three independent schools in California and Arizona, most recently at St. Gregory College Preparatory School in Tucson.

Other Eye On Education Books Available from Routledge

(www.routledge.com/eyeoneducaion)

Essential Truths for Principals
Danny Steele and Todd Whitaker

10 Perspectives on Innovation in Education
Edited by Jimmy Casas, Todd Whitaker, and Jeffrey Zoul

Implicit Bias in Schools: A Practitioner's Guide
Gina Laura Gullo, Kelly Capatosto, and Cheryl Staats

Sharing Your Education Expertise with the World: Make Research Resonate and Widen Your Impact
Jenny Grant Rankin

The Superintendent's Rulebook: A Guide to District-Level Leadership
Patrick Darfler-Sweeney

20 Formative Assessment Strategies that Work: A Guide Across Content and Grade Levels
Kate Wolfe Maxlow and Karen L. Sanzo

Intentional Innovation: How to Guide Risk-Taking, Build Creative Capacity, and Lead Change
A. J. Juliani

Six Steps to Boost Student Learning: A Leader's Guide
Karen A. Goeller

Data Analysis for Continuous School Improvement, 4th Edition
Victoria L. Bernhardt

Reinventing Crediting for Competency-Based Education

The Mastery Transcript Consortium Model and Beyond

Jonathan E. Martin

Routledge
Taylor & Francis Group

NEW YORK AND LONDON

First published 2020
by Routledge
52 Vanderbilt Avenue, New York, NY 10017

and by Routledge
2 Park Square, Milton Park, Abingdon, Oxon, OX14 4RN

Routledge is an imprint of the Taylor & Francis Group, an informa business

Library of Congress Cataloguing in Publication Data
A catalog record for this title has been requested

ISBN: 978-1-138-60921-1 (hbk)
ISBN: 978-1-138-60922-8 (pbk)
ISBN: 978-0-429-46625-0 (ebk)

Typeset in Joanna MT
by Swales & Willis Ltd, Exeter, Devon, UK

This is dedicated to my wife Carman, an extraordinary teacher, a wonderful, loving mother, and my everything.

Contents

Foreword

Kevin Mattingly

Riverdale Country School, and Klingenstein Center,
Teachers College, Columbia University

The term "wicked problems" entered the lexicon of organizational leadership almost fifty years ago (in a 1973 article by Horst Rittel and Melvin Webber, "Dilemmas in a General Theory of Planning," in the journal *Policy Sciences*), and has been a central concept in the field since that time. What are wicked problems? They are highly complex, often involve much uncertainty, are hard to define, have many causes, and can never be truly solved. What makes these situations particularly tough is that they frequently bring together constituencies with different value positions that do not agree about the nature of the problem. In other words, wicked problems are found whenever people come together and try to make things better.

In the book that follows, *Reinventing Crediting for Competency-Based Education*, Jonathan Martin has boldly tackled one of the educational world's increasingly urgent wicked problems—how we document and communicate student learning in the form of the traditional transcript composed of grades. It is no doubt a complicated problem, fraught with the competing interests of various stakeholders—students, teachers, parents, coaches, college admissions deans, boards, and others—all with their own values and goals, each focused for different reasons at different times on this entity called the transcript, and all probably aware—to one degree or another—that it is an inadequate and outdated educational and decision-making tool. This book is not the first to decry the anachronistic nature of the academic transcript as a communication form for student learning in terms of its ambiguity, inconsistency, reductionism, and tendency to focus students on achievement ("doing school") and high grades at the expense of deep and durable learning in transferable ways. But what this book does do is discuss at length what needs to change and how, providing plentiful models, exemplars, and suggestions for next steps.

It is a propitious time to be grappling with this set of issues. The college admissions world knows things are broken and need to be fundamentally retooled. Witness the two recent reports assembled under the guidance of the Harvard Graduate School of Education and supported by over 140 admissions deans of selective US colleges and universities (Richard Weissbourd's *Turning the Tide: Inspiring the Common Good and Concern for Others* [2016] and *Turning the Tide II: How Parents and High Schools Can Cultivate Ethical Character and Reduce Distress in the College Admissions Process* [2019]). Among other recommendations they make is to affirm the meaningful consideration and re-weighting for admission purposes of student accomplishments and commitments in addition to grades and test scores. Another promising current circumstance for traditional transcript transformation is the ongoing digital revolution, which provides the means for ePortfolios in K-12 schools to more richly, complexly, and in varied formats capture and convey student learning, both for within-school student growth, but also as a way to convey student learning to admissions teams and employers. The newly formed Mastery Transcript Consortium, discussed in detail in this book, is one example of this sort of initiative, and now involves several hundred schools around the country. In addition, current conceptions of twenty-first-century learning goals are another change enhancer (e.g. P21, Hewlett's Deeper Learning), expanding the notion of "what's worth learning" beyond the purely academic into character qualities and the social-emotional realms, and into life beyond the confines of academia, none of which can be captured in the traditional transcript in readily interpretable forms. The ground is fertile for change.

That said, few people I know in the educational world are as well-equipped as the author of this book to struggle with this enormously complex set of issues just described. Jonathan Martin's experiences in the realm of learning are extensive and varied, including being a classroom teacher, leader of multiple schools, think-tank researcher, published writer, prolific blogger, and consultant to numerous schools and national educational organizations—an academic polymath if there ever was one. He possesses an extraordinary ability to distill and synthesize information from disparate sources and cohere them into unique and compelling insights, and this stands him in good stead in weaving his way through this tangled educational thicket. My own introduction and initial understanding of these issues began in the late 1980s when introduced to the writings of Grant

Wiggins and then later working with him in various capacities for many years. About the same time I began to teach in the professional development programs of the Klingenstein Center at Teachers College Columbia University, and I have been teaching cognitive science in their graduate leadership programs for the past twenty years, having the good fortune to interact with hundreds of extraordinary educators during that time. So I do not say lightly, nor without cause, that Jonathan is among the best of them. In Lee Shulman terms, he embodies the "wisdom of practice."

This book is quintessentially about moving forward in productive and positive ways in the face of one of education's most daunting wicked problems. Central to the author's argument is the concept of the competency-based credit (CBC), which is carefully differentiated from competency-based learning (CBL) and competency-based education (CBE), both powerful and growing reform movements in teaching and learning. As discussed in the book, a CBC provides credit for student performances that demonstrate competency or mastery of specifically defined and articulated learning goals achieved through some form of performance-based assessment (i.e. application, use, transfer, creation). Credit is not given for simply passing a course or for "seat time" in terms of class attendance. In addition, the quality of a performance is judged against clear, rigorous, and specific rubrics applied by trained reviewers; the use of formative feedback by the student is key; student reflection is integral; and, student work and assessment are curated in ePortfolios or a learning management system (LMS). Functional adherence to the CBC concept, therefore, assures that student credits directly reflect student learning in enduring and transferable ways. This is transformative and revolutionary.

It is also operationally very difficult. Fortunately, the remainder of the book is a thoughtful treatise on the challenges and potential obstacles along the way to rethinking and redesigning the way we communicate student learning, both for student growth purposes within schools to students and teachers (including assessment and instructional strategies), and for communicating student learning outside schools to parents, colleges, and employers. The author has done an excellent job at each major juncture of the process in providing relevant essential questions, surfacing hidden assumptions, anticipating obstacles, and describing real-world examples to guide the way. It's still a wicked problem but as the change leadership gurus suggest, a first move in effecting change in complex systems is to identify and begin to consider all the issues at play. This book certainly goes a long way to accomplishing that.

Meet the Author

Jonathan E. Martin has consulted to schools and educational organizations since 2012, and currently directs professional learning for a leading global nonprofit assessment and learning organization. Among his recent client organizations are the Mastery Transcript Consortium, EdLeader21, National Association of Independent Schools, Enrollment Management Association, Blackbaud, INDEX, Think Through Math, and dozens of schools in the US and Mexico. From 1996 to 2012 he served as Head of School at three independent schools in California and Arizona. He holds degrees from Harvard University (BA), and the University of San Francisco (MA, School Administration). Find more of his writing and publications at his blog, www.21k12blog.org.

Acknowledgments

In January 2016, two school-leader friends and consulting clients—Tim Bazemore of Catlin Gabel School and Nanci Kauffman of Castilleja School—told me of a new endeavor they were supporting to re-invent the high school transcript, and encouraged me to attend that endeavor's first meeting that coming spring. Soon thereafter, I received a warm invitation from the initiative's founder, Hawken School Head of School Scott Looney. As a result, in 2016 and 2017, I participated in early foundational work for the Mastery Transcript Consortium (MTC) by participating in launch events in Cleveland (April 2016) and San Francisco (March 2017); preparing, at Scott's request, sample "mastery" rubrics that were distributed to MTC member schools in 2017; and spending two days in July 2017 to develop an agenda and training materials for the upcoming school MTC Site Director meetings with six extraordinary educators and thought leaders: Scott Looney, Trish Russell, Kevin Mattingly, Eric Hudson, Nicole Furlonge, and Nigel Furlonge. That summer, I also prepared two documents for the MTC: a sample set of mastery credits and a comprehensive change management plan, both of which were distributed to the MTC Site Director meetings in 2017 and 2018. I'm deeply appreciative of Scott and MTC Interim Executive Director Trish Russell for including me so kindly in the early phase of developing key components of the MTC.

This is not, however, a book about the Mastery Transcript Consortium itself. It does feature a chapter about the MTC, but, that chapter aside, this book is intended to address the wider model of competency-based crediting and transcripts that MTC exemplifies. This inquiry is intended to inform and support equally the work of educators working within the MTC and those working on other, analogous competency-based crediting innovation efforts. Important to note: the book and I have no affiliation with the MTC organization. MTC staff had no involvement in its preparation, did not review any of its content, and have no responsibility for anything written here. This book does not purport to speak for or represent the MTC. I am solely responsible for what's written.

There are very many educators and colleagues from whom and with whom I've learned so much during my thirty years in K-12 education, only some of whom I can include in this partial listing. In addition to the aforementioned, in no particular order, they are: Michelle Berry, Rich Roberts, Jeremy Burrus, Julie Wilson, Bob Pearlman, Simmy Ziv-El, Rick Belding, Scott Morris, Bernie Trilling, Charles Fadel, Suzanne Conquest, Bryan Williams, Vinnie Vrotny, Alex Inman, Ben Daley, John Gulla, Olaf Jorgenson, Rick Ackerley, Chris Bigenho, Chris Thinnes, Marsha Little, Brett Jacobsen, Richard Whitmore, Brian Thomas, Jason Ravitz, Amada Torres, Eric Juli, Eric Temple, Dave Monaco, Mark Hale, Brandon Dorman, Jamie Baker, Landis Green, Richard Kassissieh, Vincent Hermosilla, Howard Levin, Karen Stroble, Marjorie Mitchell, Dominic Randolph, Matt Teller, Doug Lyons, Peter Gow, Corinne Dedini, Brad Rathgeber, Eve Rifkin, Carrie Brennan, Brett Goble, JoAnn Groh, Santo Nicotera, Tim Grivois-Shah, Bob Ryshke, Max McConkey, Laura Deisley, Chris Lehmann, Pam Moran, Ira Socol, John Merrow, the late Tom Little, Paul Chapman, Ariane Solwell, Seth Solwell, Stan Cardinet, Gretchen Griswold, Kate Haber, Dave Kinstle, Mike Golston, Susan Heintz, Heather Faircloth, Will Bladt, Chris LaBonte, Amy Sullivan, Lisa Pullman, Jefferson Burnett, Pat Bassett, Tyler Thigpen, Bo Adams, Grant Lichtman, Carla Silver, Mark Silver, Greg Bamford, Rhonda Durham, Thomas Steele-Maley, Tom Farquhar, Glenn Whitman, Heather Hoerle, Nicole Suozzi, Michael Ulku-Steiner, Ray Diffley, Mike Hanas, Hadley Ferguson, Kim Sivick, T.J. Locke, Lee Quinby, Judy Lucas, Halsey Bell, Emily McCarren, Orpheus Crutchfield, Jeneen Graham, Mark Crotty, Mark Desjardins, Nancy Hayes, John Bracker, Sharon Thompson, Jim McManus, Mary Fauvre, Joel Weiss, Lindsey Gilbert, Mike Gwaltney, Jim Tracy, Nasif Iskander, Bryan Williams, Michael Thompson, Rob Hereford, Tony Wagner, Ken Kay, Valerie Greenhill, George Couros, Lyn Hilt, Will Richardson, Lisa Thumann, Liz Davis, Jonathan Howland, Zach Lehman, Patrick Larkin, Chris Jackson, Elizabeth Helfant, Connie White, Suzie Boss. Thanks also go to my friendly hosts in New Zealand, including Richard Wells, Claire Amos, Karen Spencer, Justine Monroe, and Faye Langdon.

I want to extend appreciation to the staff of Tucson's Lodge on the Desert, who showed me warm hospitality as I retreated to this lovely site for many writer's weekends in Summer and Fall 2018. Warm thoughts go to my "co-workers" at downtown Tucson's Connect Co-Working space, who have provided me with kind professional and personal colleagueship for my workdays since 2015.

Big thanks to Kevin Mattingly, whom I've long held in the highest regard for his thoughtfulness and expertise about educational excellence and curricular innovation, for reading this carefully, providing me many notes, and writing the Foreword. Thanks also to Routledge's Dan Schwartz for his excellent support as editor.

I'm extraordinarily fortunate to have always had the greatest of support and love from my parents, grandparents, and siblings. My kids—Rhea and Nate—are my pride and joy, and watching closely their secondary school experience has informed many of my thoughts and beliefs about the long-overdue transformation of secondary schooling that will benefit all high school students in the future.

1

Introduction

Consider how few inventions from the late nineteenth century we continue to use, and how few we will be using for much longer. We're fast phasing out the use of coal-powered electrical generation, the internal combustion engine, the landline telephone, and the incandescent light bulb.

It's time, too, to look at phasing out the traditional high school transcript, the one-page piece of paper listing courses completed and letter grades earned, the one utilizing Carnegie Units. It's time—long past time—to award students credits for demonstrated proficiency, not for time spent sitting in chairs. Learning should become the constant, time the variable.

This transition is the natural order of things. Products follow a predictable pattern of introduction, growth, and then a long, stable maturity—before they begin their inevitable decline. This time is coming for the traditional transcript and the Carnegie or "standard unit." It probably can't last much longer, what with its intrinsic limitations and more importantly the rising tide of innovations coming to challenge it with new aspirations and new technologies. But rather than simply awaiting its inevitable demise, today many educators are joining together to ideate, innovate, and implement successor systems to the conventional transcript and crediting for secondary school learning.

This alternative model is what we call crediting for competencies earned through demonstrated proficiency or mastery, rather than crediting for courses completed by "time in seats." Seeing it as an extension of competency-based education (CBE), we'll call this alternative form of transcript and crediting "competency-based crediting"

(CBC), while acknowledging that the terminology is still slippery, and some call this mastery learning or mastery-based or proficiency-based crediting. One prominent example of this new model is the "Mastery Transcript" as defined by the Mastery Transcript Consortium (MTC); the MTC calls this a "mastery credit" system.

Here in Chapter 1, we'll look at why and why now this change is coming, what it entails, and what it looks like.

Why Competency-Based Crediting, and Why Now?

Concerns and critiques about the conventional high school transcript and the standardized course crediting are hardly new. They have regularly appeared in the 120-odd years since its adoption around the turn of the twentieth century. More than sixty years ago, in 1954, the US Department of Health, Education, and Welfare's Office of Education published a monograph entitled *The Carnegie Unit: its Origin, Status, and Trends*. Contemporary readers of this monograph will quickly recognize the timelessness of many of our current concerns about the conventional high school crediting system and transcript:

1. It encourages a rigid schedule of classes and subjects, which makes needed innovations in the high school program difficult.
2. It gives undue emphasis to the time served, to subjects and to textbooks, without appropriate emphasis on [the] amount learned in subjects.
3. It fosters the assumption that all pupils can acquire the same minimum amount of learning or subject mastery in a given period of time, thus encouraging well endowed pupils to loaf and requiring those less well endowed to attempt to achieve the impossible and thus suffer possible failure.
4. It provides no uniform means for measuring such qualitative learnings as social adjustment, moral and ethical development, leadership, attitudes, work experience, civic competence, and a variety of other essential and valuable human objectives.

(Tomkins & Gaumnitz, 1954)

Today, though, we are seeing a great increase in attention to the limitations of the standard credit and transcript, and many are declaring it is time for a new approach.

Why now?

1. Things are broken that need fixing; the status quo is increasingly untenable.
2. Aspirations are rising for better aligning student credits and records for the values we have in twenty-first-century learning.
3. New models and technologies are making the shift easier to imagine, design, implement, and manage.

Problems and Limitations of the Status Quo

The greatest driver of change may be the rising dissatisfaction of educators, parents, colleges, employers, and students themselves. The limitations and deficiencies of the contemporary high school transcript are passing the tipping point. Though these limitations are many, some stand out.

Grade inflation has been increasing annually since the sixties, just as our currency has seen inflation. Average grades have risen dramatically, and letter grades no longer allow colleges or employers to meaningfully discriminate among the top third, roughly, of the graduating classes at many high schools. *Inside Higher Ed* reports on a recent College Board study finding that looking at cohorts of high school graduates who finished from 1998 to 2016, the average high school GPA went up from 3.27 to 3.38: "The data come both from the Education Department and from surveys the College Board conducts of students who take the SAT" (Jaschik, 2017).

And the problem is especially true at certain types of schools; the rate has been "more than twice that at private, nonreligious schools. The percentage of seniors claiming to have an A average has also risen, from 39 percent to 47 percent" (Murphy, 2017).

But this is only half the problem. When grades are inflated in systems that reinforce grading as the primary driver of certifying preparation, students feel forced to compete and stress over the littlest things, beseeching teachers for extra points, disputing every demerit, striving to be credited for compliance, not for the real work of mastering challenging material.

Stanford Professor of Education Denise Pope's *Doing School* is an acutely observed narrative of a high-achieving, highly competitive public high school. The book:

> follows five highly regarded students through a school year and discovers that these young people believe getting ahead requires manipulating the system, scheming, lying, and cheating. They feel that in order to get ahead they must compromise their values. In short, they "do school"—that is, they are not really engaged with learning nor can they commit to such values as integrity and community.
>
> (Pope, 2003)

It should be said that Pope doesn't blame students for their choices, nor do we in this book: students act in these ways because their options are so limited, and the system is structured so that this is what is defined for them as success, and other pathways toward more authentic and ultimately more sustained and meaningful learning simply aren't available to them.

Pope wrote that more than a decade ago; she reiterated these concerns when being quoted in a recent magazine article:

> [Students] realize that they are caught in a system where achievement depends more on "doing"—going through the correct motions—than on learning and engaging with the curriculum. Instead of thinking deeply about the content of their courses and delving into projects and assignments, the students focus on managing the workload and honing strategies that will help them to achieve high grades.
>
> (Looney, 2017)

Meanwhile, in other schools, particularly where resources are poorer, many students are passed along for cooperation and good citizenship, while their grades lack any connection to actual mastery of material. As educational writer Rose Colby notes in her book *Competency-Based Education*:

> Our colleges and business have no way to tell from current school transcripts if students have met performance criteria for graduation. In addition, the course content from one high school to another can vary greatly, and the lack of performance criteria in granting credit

for courses has eroded the value and meaning of the high school diploma. . . . Schools need to rethink the notion that credit accrual alone translates into competence and college and career readiness.

(Colby, 2017)

What letter grades really mean—what they are pegged to beyond any individual teacher's opinion—has been a longstanding problem. Grant Wiggins, renowned late author of *Understanding by Design* and one of our most thoughtful education writers, observed this back in 1989. "An 'A' in English means only that some adult thought the student's work was excellent. Compared to what or whom? As determined by what criteria? In reference to what specific subject matter?" (Wiggins, 1989).

New Aspirations

Across many sectors, our nation has embraced so-called twenty-first-century skills such as critical thinking, communication, collaboration, and creativity. Not new to the world, they are far more important for a far greater proportion of the workforce than ever before. Even the most elite professionals must now work together to solve problems, interpret data, and offer value beyond what can be provided by the performance of intelligent machines. Our schools must not only integrate these essential skills but develop a system of accountability for their mastery. Today, these skills tend to buried under the "content" of the curriculum of, for instance, US History or Biology, and recognition of them in assessment is diluted by an emphasis on testing and factual recall. Educators need to ensure that students have the opportunity to learn these skills, and learn them deeply and lastingly, for transfer and application, not just for short-term performance.

Fortunately, there is rising interest in allowing and empowering students to showcase these crucial skills—critical thinking and communication, for instance, and also global competency, meta-cognition, and creative problem-solving—and the breadth of the things they've accomplished, the skills they've mastered, on their transcripts. If this critical document and record is to be a key ticket to the future, a passport to post-secondary learning and professional opportunities, shouldn't it report more than just the courses taken and grades awarded? In a 2018 piece on *Education Week*, educational innovation observer Tom Vander Ark writes about the potential value in transcripts that "help students share personal bests, unique accomplishments and capabilities, and evidence of growth on career readiness indicators" (Vander Ark, 2018). He also writes that, in the conventional form:

> Narrow focus on course and credit requirements limits emphasis on the importance of out-of-school learning (for example work, service, and civic-based learning). There are few if any opportunities to gain credit for out-of-school or informal learning (learning fractions on Khan Academy, taking calculus on a MOOC [Massive Open Online Course], starting one's on business or cause).
>
> (Vander Ark, 2018)

There is also a growing embrace of what is called "performance assessment." In order to attain a driver's license, one must first pass a multiple-choice test, but that is not all that is required: the real test comes on the road, in real-world circumstances, while actually performing the task the test is certifying. The same should be true for schooling at every level. Doctorate students produce some kind of thesis to demonstrate their capacity to do the work of the field in which they are earning degrees. Road driving tests, dissertations: these are examples of performance assessments, and, increasingly, we are seeing them called for in secondary education. In New York state, schools can opt out of the state Regents exam and have their aspiring graduates demonstrate their skill sets with a performance task project culminating in an exhibition. Innovative charter and public school programs such as High Tech High, New Tech Network, and Science Leadership Academy require students to prepare and present portfolios of completed work in independent projects that demand careful preparation and thorough mastery of the knowledge and skills involved. Stanford's SCALE—Stanford Center for Assessment, Learning, and Equity—is both a cause of and a response to this rising demand for performance assessments, and its comprehensive website is complete with design guidance and example performance tasks in every subject area.

Performance assessment can and should be utilized in conventional high school courses. But it can be far richer when it asks students to go beyond the confines of a single subject, when it asks and demands of them the integration of skills and knowledge from multiple disciplines. Most higher academic performances—and most professional performances—entail synthesizing skills of literacy and numeracy, of drawing upon historical knowledge and technical understanding, and the ability to apply these multiple strands to a novel challenge. Life isn't lived inside narrow subject area disciplines, and truly challenging problems are rarely situated exclusively within the abstractions of a single class or course. Students too often find learning artificial, airless, and narrow as they race down crowded hallways every 45 minutes to shift gears from quadratic equations to the origins of World War II to the use of the present participle to the periodic table, all of it in a vacuum separate from the dynamic demands of the world just outside the school doors. High-quality performance assessment will better enable teachers to provide and demand of students this type of more extended, applied, and multidisciplinary learning.

Performance assessment cannot be rendered especially effectively into letter grades and traditional course crediting; there is always a loss of information and substance when one tries to squeeze and shape the complexity and richness of performance assessment and interdisciplinary learning into a Carnegie unit format—into simple, single-course credits. As we shall see, a primary motivation for the launch of the Mastery Transcript Consortium came from challenges that one school's leadership confronted after creating an entrepreneurship studies program, entailing powerful learning in real-world settings that included economics study and internships. In the eyes of students and teachers, as was recounted by MTC founder Looney, this course "counted" for a lot, far more than most traditional courses, but it couldn't easily be counted on a transcript in Carnegie units (Looney, 2017).

One more aspirational "pull" is a fast-growing appreciation for the extraordinary diversity of learners in our schools. The Carnegie unit, which awards three credits for the completion of a year-long course in about 120 hours, is designed to recognize the learning of "average" students. Author Todd Rose recently explained that there is no such thing as an average student; his book proclaims in its title that we are seeing *The End of Average: How We Succeed in a World that Values Sameness*. It is time, he writes, that we all begin "refusing to be caged in by arbitrary, average-based pronouncements of who we are expected to be" (Rose, 2017). Some students learn much faster than the average, and others learn more slowly; to award credits for 60 or 120 seat hours seems silly when you think about it this way. But it is not just a matter of undoing seat time because of pacing issues. Students benefit from different scaffolding and sequencing of learning; some will prefer to accumulate credits for graduation with more specialization, like college students do, or with different mixtures of content knowledge acquisition, skill development, and application. Today's transcript and crediting model is too rigid to accommodate the diversity of learning we know exists.

Opportunities: Technologies and Models

Meanwhile, new technologies and models are making new approaches such as competency-based education and crediting more feasible.

Though still far from universal in education reform, standards-based grading (SBG) has dramatically risen in the awareness and practice of educators; Google Trends reveals a tenfold increase in searches for the term across the past decade. Even in the many schools that have no official policy or formal SBG practice, it has entered conversation on a more regular basis; educators are considering how they can design grading not to collect and average test scores but to establish whether key course criteria for learning have been met. SBG is not competency-based learning or grading, but it can be a valuable prerequisite in the professional journey of many educators and educational systems, helping them to recognize the way course completion ought to be built upon demonstrated learning of key intended outcomes, not just seat time.

In other sectors, badging and micro-credentials have become popularized. Nearly everyone is familiar with the idea of badging among the Boy Scouts and Girl Scouts. For nearly a century, Scouts have organized learning and achievement into a simple, intuitive, and easy-to-track format. The organization identifies skills that would be valuable for young people's development, establishes clear criteria for demonstration of competency, and, upon the completion of tasks that meet those criteria, award a badge. Only some badges are required for progression through the ranks, but many are available, allowing young people to choose how they wish to advance through the ranks and, upon earning the required number and completing a major project, gain what is in effect a quasi-graduation or diploma, the Eagle Scout accomplishment.

The model of scout badging is a clear inspiration and template for the competency-based crediting shift that this book will explore. Digital learning environments have, in the past decade or so, fast expanded the use of badges to certify proficiencies in an enormous array of areas.

A digital badge is a validated indicator of accomplishment, skill, quality, or interest that can be earned in many learning environments. Open digital badging makes it easy for anyone to issue, earn, and display badges across the web—through an infrastructure that uses shared and open technical technical standards. The world is changing fast and, today more than ever, traditional modes of assessment fail to capture the learning that happens everywhere and at every age. Digital badges are a powerful new tool for identifying and validating the rich array of people's skills, knowledge, accomplishments, and competencies. Digital badges inspire new pathways to learning and connect learners to opportunities, resources, and one another.

(Digital Badges, n.d.)

David Niguidula, in his book *Demonstrating Student Mastery with Digital Badges and Portfolios*, summarizes the many ways digital badges offer many strengths, including filling in for the deficits of standardized tests, providing incentives for student acquisition of specialized skills, and recognition of how learning can and does span many contexts, including those outside the schoolhouse (Niguidula, 2019).

Technology is making student portfolios of work more easily collected and managed, and allowing for new forms of transcripts that previously would have been impossible. A conventional transcript can easily be rendered on a single piece of paper —it is something every reader can probably picture in their heads. On the left, organized into grades nine through twelve, courses are listed such as English 9, US History, and Algebra 1; on the right there might be two columns, one for each semester, perhaps divided into two parts, one for a letter grade and one for a number of credits earned. That's it: simple and straightforward. But think, too, about the very fact of that simplicity: what is a feature of the transcript is also a bug. It captures and conveys so little information. Our goal is to improve the quantity and quality of information without sacrificing the simplicity, and technology can help.

Digital portfolios can now contain huge amounts of information and curate or organize that data into visually compelling, color-coded displays and dashboards. Reviewers can easily see summaries and, with a tap, dig deeper for further supporting evidence. The Lumina Foundation has been providing grants to colleges and universities to develop such tools, responding to the demand from colleges. For example, Thomas

Black, former registrar and associate vice provost for student affairs at Stanford, refers to the current transcript as "a record of everything the student has forgotten," and asserts, "There's a clamor, for something more meaningful" (Schneider, 2015). Katherine Mangan lays out some ideas:

> That "something" is a form of extended transcript or digital portfolio that captures more of what students are learning both inside and outside the classroom. There could be links for study abroad and internships, robotics competitions and volunteer activities. An electronic portfolio could include examples of creative writing or artwork, or an engineering prototype a student developed. And at a time when everyone, it seems, is looking for evidence of "competencies," students could highlight the specific learning outcomes they gained in their courses.
>
> (Schneider, 2015)

For a terrific treatment of how the skillful combination of digital portfolios, competency-based educational practices, and digital badges can establish an effective structure for competency-based crediting, see the aforementioned *Demonstrating Student Mastery* book by Niguidula. As he writes in his book's conclusion:

> Digital badges can be a powerful way to show student progress toward a school's goals; collecting the evidence behind those badges into digital portfolios provides a unique insight into each student and to the tasks they have done to reach this point.
>
> (Niguidula, 2019)

Competency-Based Crediting

The limitations of the current model, the greater aspirations educators have for their students, and new technologies and techniques that are increasingly available: all are coming together to make this moment the time for a new kind of crediting system and transcript, one we're calling competency-based crediting.

CBC draws heavily on the educational project called competency-based education, CBE (sometimes called competency-based learning, or CBL). But CBC and CBE are not the same.

CBE is defined by the website CompetencyWorks as "a systems model in which (1) teaching and learning are designed to ensure students are becoming proficient by advancing on demonstrated mastery and (2) schools are organized to provide timely and differentiated support to ensure equity" (Competency Education, n.d.).

The CompetencyWorks website explains that in 2011, experts came together and established the following as key CBE components:

- Students advance upon demonstrated mastery.
- Competencies include explicit, measurable, transferable learning objectives that empower students.
- Assessment is meaningful and a positive learning experience for students.
- Students receive timely, differentiated support based on their individual learning needs.
- Learning outcomes emphasize competencies that include application and creation of knowledge, along with the development of important skills and dispositions.

(Competency Education, n.d.)

Competency-based crediting entails the use of all of the above components, and then goes beyond to credit students' mastery of competencies, not course completion. To draw the distinction, many CBE models require completion of a traditional set of courses, and provide credits only for course completion. The course credits themselves are earned on a competency basis but the diploma is earned only upon the completion of a defined number of conventional courses, recorded on a traditional transcript.

To illustrate the gap between CBE and CBC, we can look to an article written in 2016 by Brian Stack, principal of Sanborn High School in New Hampshire. His school is among the most interesting and impressive CBE schools in the country, and his leadership there is praiseworthy. In his piece, entitled "Separating the Facts from the Myths in the Competency-Based High School Transcript," he writes that, even in a fully developed CBE program, "the role of the transcript has not changed, and its format doesn't have to either" (Stack, 2016). Responding to the "myth" that a competency-based education transcript is too long and too confusing, Stack says: "Most competency-based [education] high school transcripts still contain the same base reporting measures, which include course names, final course grades, credit earned, grade point average, and class rank" (Stack, 2016).

Regarding college admissions officers who review competency-based educational transcripts such as his own, Stack says, "I have yet to encounter one who was confused by our transcript or our competency-based reporting model" (Stack, 2016). But, when confronting the limitations and even the crisis of the contemporary transcript, educators calling for reform actually desire there be some momentary confusion or temporary disequilibrium in the college ranks. As Piaget taught us, disequilibrium is a necessary phase in the journey toward greater under-standing; without it, there will be no meaningful change from the status quo to a new reality.

A definition of CBC then would include all that is in the CBE definition above, with the addition that:

- Demonstrated mastery/competency, not conventional course com-pletion, is what is credited in school, and these competencies are recorded on transcripts and communicated in comprehensive and carefully delineated ways.

Because these competencies are what count for the high stakes of meeting graduation requirements and being evaluated for admission and hiring, CBC usually also entails:

- Additional emphasis on the aforementioned high standards for students demonstrating and earning credit, such as transfer, application, and creation.
- Rigorous assessment of student work products, using validated rubrics and panels of trained educators or external reviewers.
- Student work carefully curated in portfolios available for review by external evaluators.
- An enhanced attention to the role of formative assessment and student reflection throughout the learning and crediting process.

Structure of the Book

The remainder of this book, after this first introductory section, addresses the following:

Chapters 2, 3, and 4: What Does a Competency-Based Crediting System Look Like and Entail?

What does CBC look like in practice, and what components does it contain? We'll begin this section by looking in Chapter 2 at three exemplary models: a post-secondary example, Western Governors University; a graduate school example, Lerner Medical College; and a comprehensive secondary school CBC system used universally in New Zealand. Next, we'll look in Chapter 3 closely at the Mastery Transcript Consortium: its origins, vision, process, and promise. Chapter 4 then will unpack and explain key components of a CBC system, including the work of defining competencies, earning and awarding competencies, the assembly of student work into portfolios, and then the transcript itself.

Chapter 5. Downstream Effects: What Will This Mean for Secondary Curriculum, Instruction, and Assessment?

CBC can and will have far-reaching, transformative impact on curriculum, instruction, and classroom assessment. Where, when, and how students are credited for their learning will all change, and the role of the teacher will change. Although it will be impossible to be exhaustive, Chapter 5 will review and discuss some of these "downstream" impacts.

Chapters 6 and 7: How Does Change Happen, Where Do I Start, and How Do I Plan Such a Shift?

Perhaps the most important aspect of this book is not the why or the what but the how: How do educators—school leaders, board members, and teachers—work toward advancing CBC? Chapter 6 will provide seven short case studies of this kind of transformation at schools that have completed, or begun to undertake, the work. It will also identify seven lessons to learn from these case studies. Chapter 7 then will provide a thorough set of sequential steps and strategies for leading schools and districts toward a shift to CBC. This discussion will be action-oriented, grounded in concrete steps, and carefully arranged to make for effective leadership and change.

Chapters 8 and 9: The View from Higher Education, and Considerations for Advancing the Work

As the book comes to its conclusion, we'll recognize and respond to concerns of critiques of this new approach coming from higher ed and elsewhere. We'll also identify key takeaways and considerations for the future of CBC.

One View of a CBC Future

Arriving at school at 8:45 Monday morning, Yolanda enters the learning commons and opens her laptop to plan her week. She knows her first priority is to prepare for her English seminar, beginning at 9:30; she has to review the Lady Macbeth sleepwalking scene and form the talking points she will present in class for her interpretation of its implications. But before she does, she takes a moment to reflect on the differences between her current and previous learning experiences. Before, school began at 7:30 and often felt like a forced march through a jam-packed day of listening to teachers talk with little time for reflection upon or consolidation about what she is learning, and even less for critical thinking and creativity.

Shakespeare seminar runs 9:30 to 10:45. Before the semester began, she met with her teacher and identified the literacy competencies she wanted to focus on and the credits for those competencies she sought to achieve; they determined that literary analysis and oral argumentation would be the two to strive for. Today in class she will be able to practice and demonstrate her growing skills in each as she debates her classmates on the significance of Lady Macbeth's handwashing. The debate goes reasonably well, and afterwards she composes a short reflection on her performance making reference to the literary analysis rubric which defines proficiency for this competency, which will be included in her portfolio. Later that afternoon, her teacher will also respond to her reflection using the online management system, provide her feedback, and note the particular subskills of analysis and argumentation that Yolanda displayed. After Yolanda completes a revision of her piece based on that feedback, both her reflection and the teacher note will be entered in her portfolio and tagged for easy access and organization.

After a fifteen-minute break, Yolanda spends the next forty-five minutes in the Media Center working on Math. She is using Khan Academy to work her way at her own pace through PreCalculus, earning badges along the way, which she'll enter into her portfolio, tagged for her Mathematical Analysis Competency credit. When encountering difficulties, she is easily able to access a math learning coach, but sometimes she prefers first to confer with schoolmates also at work in this space.

Lunch is a working session today, with one of the school's science teachers. Yolanda is interning in a science research facility fifteen miles away. She spends every Tuesday working with chemists formulating new pharmaceuticals. This work is intended to earn her credits in both scientific research and knowledge competencies, but her teacher and lab supervisor is concerned that she isn't being diligent enough in reading the scientific study binders the lab has provided and has not demonstrated a core understanding of the underlying conceptual principles for the research in her journal. Over lunch, the teacher counsels Yolanda that she needs to give this more attention, and improve her journaling, or her credits here might be delayed or at risk.

Lunch completed, and warning received, Yolanda heads upstairs to a large conference room where furnishings are flexibly arranged into about a dozen groups of five or six seats. Here, she joins her team for the afternoon, one of three full afternoons this week (two on campus and one downtown inside a local community agency) that she'll spend working with them on a year-long interdisciplinary community impact project. She and her team, reporting to a small group of teacher-facilitators, have determined that this project should result in competency credits for historical research and analysis, statistics, financial literacy, and for conscientiousness: persistence and organization. Using a design thinking protocol, they began by interviewing residents of a nearby neighborhood "food desert," and then prepared a report on the historical events nationally and regionally that resulted in this circumstance, complete with statistical analysis of comparative healthy food access in different neighborhoods in their metropolitan area. The report required them to do a month-long study of US History, and they worked closely with one of their facilitators, a math teacher, on getting the statistical analysis to work well, sometimes going to online statistics video lessons and websites to understand better their task. She isn't entirely looking forward to presenting the report, because public speaking to unfamiliar adults stresses her, but she thinks they are on track to success when they share their report, using a Powerpoint and question-and-answer session, with a community planning board in her city next month.

Arriving home, Yolanda isn't done. She has a couple of hours of work ahead of her, most of it for her passion project, which at this school will be recognized on her transcript: managing the school newspaper. For this, she'll eventually earn competency credits for writing skills and collaboration.

She also needs to spend an hour on Rosetta Stone, working on her Spanish skills, a study that will culminate in a world language competency credit.

This is what schooling can and should be. Competency-based crediting can support the transition of secondary school to one of greater personalization, greater student agency, greater authenticity, and ultimately greater and deeper learning.

References

Colby, R. (2017). *Competency-Based Education: A New Architecture for K-12 Schooling.* Cambridge, MA: Harvard Education Press.

Competency Education (n.d.). CompetencyWorks. Retrieved September 13, 2018, from www.competencyworks.org/about/competency-education/

Digital Badges (n.d.). Retrieved September 13, 2018, from www.hastac.org/initiatives/digital-badges

Jaschik, S. (2017, July 17). High School Grades: Higher and Higher. *Inside Higher Ed.* Retrieved September 13, 2018, from www.insidehighered.com/admissions/article/2017/07/17/study-finds-notable-increase-grades-high-schools-nationally

Looney, S. (2017, September 11). Independent Schools Come Together to Build a New High School Transcript. Retrieved September 13, 2018, from www.nais.org/learn/independent-ideas/september-2017/independent-schools-come-together-to-build-a-new-high-school-transcript-(1)

Murphy, J. (2017, September 15). An Analysis of the College Board's Study on Grade Inflation (essay). *Inside Higher Ed.* Retrieved September 13, 2018, from www.insidehighered.com/views/2017/09/15/analysis-college-boards-study-grade-inflation-essay

Niguidula, D. A. (2019). *Demonstrating Student Mastery with Digital Badges and Portfolios.* Alexandria, VA: ASCD.

Pope, D. (2003). *Doing school: How We Are Creating a Generation of Stressed Out, Materialistic, and Miseducated Students.* New Haven, CT: Yale University Press.

Rose, T. (2017). *The End of Average: How We Succeed in a World That Values Sameness.* London, UK: Penguin Books.

Schneider, C. (2015, July 20). It's Time to Build a Better Transcript. Retrieved September 13, 2018, from http://www.gettingsmart.com/2015/07/its-time-to-build-a-better-transcript/

Silva, E., White, T., & Toch, T. (2015). *The Carnegie Unit: A Century-Old Standard in a Changing Education Landscape* (Report). Stanford, CA: Carnegie Foundation for the Advancement of Teaching.

Stack, B. (2016, September 12). Separating the Facts from the Myths in the Competency-Based High School Transcript. Competency Works. Retrieved September 13, 2018, from www.competencyworks.org/understanding-competency-education/separating-the-facts-from-the-myths-in-the-competency-based-high-school-transcript/Schneider, C. (2015, July 20). It's Time to Build a Better Transcript. Retrieved September 13, 2018, from www.gettingsmart. com/2015/07/its-time-to-build-a-better-transcript/

Tomkins, E. & Gaumnitz, W. (1954). *The Carnegie Unit: Its Origin, Status, and Trends* Washington, DC: US Department of Health, Education, and Welfare, Office of Education.

Vander Ark, T. (2018, May 3). Rethinking the High School Credential. Retrieved September 13, 2018, from http://blogs.edweek.org/edweek/on_innovation/ 2018/05/rethinking_the_high_school_credential.html

Wiggins, G. (1989). Teaching to the Authentic Test. *Educational Leadership*, 46(7), 41–47.

2

Competency-Based Crediting Models from Higher Ed and Abroad

If competency-based crediting has so much to offer, the reader may be wondering, why doesn't it already exist on this large and diverse planet we inhabit? It does. Three models are explored: two come from higher ed, Western Governors University and Lerner Medical College, and one from secondary schooling, the NCEA system found in New Zealand. There's much to learn from their experiences, their success and accomplishments; there's even more to learn from the challenges they've encountered and the flaws in their fully implemented systems. There's nothing easy about this work, and there are many ways in which it can go awry.

Western Governors University

Western Governors University (WGU) was founded in the mid-nineties by a coalition of Governors of western US states. An entirely online university, WGU was designed for the purpose of serving working adults seeking bachelors or masters degrees for largely occupational and vocational purposes. It is among a set of mostly online universities that have built competency-based crediting models, and its approach is among the most comprehensive and complete. Unlike many other online universities, WGU is nonprofit; despite its name, it is a private, nongovernmental organization (Western Governors University, 2018).

As explained by Heather Staker, students entering WGU are required to choose a major immediately, which places them right into a course of study leading to their selected degree. However, there are no courses per se, listed or required for WGU majors, nor is there a prescribed sequence.

Students have no schedule of classes, be they synchronous or asynchronous, to which they must adhere. There is also no timeline for how long a student must study, nor a maximum amount of credits that can be earned in a given period of time. Students can actually earn credits without taking a course, if desired, by jumping directly to the assessment and demonstrating proficiency. Finally, tuition is not charged per course nor per credit, but only per six-month period of study. While many students follow a conventional timeline of three or four years to complete a bachelor's and end up paying a total tuition comparable to that of a state university, some students accelerate their credit accumulation via successful assessments at a rapid rate, and earn their degrees in just six months—or, as in one example, two degrees, both a BA and MA. Even in this example, the student pays only the one six-month tuition bill. (Whether this student also acquired deep and lasting understanding of the fields in which these degrees were earned is a separate question.) Staker calls this an "all-you-can-eat" model of tuition costing. For motivated, well-prepared, and skilled-in-learning students, WGU appears to offer a highly affordable and time-efficient alternative to a traditional education (Staker, 2012).

Each major contains several domains, divided into several competencies, which in turn are divided in multiple specific objectives. To earn a competency, students must demonstrate proficiency in the objectives, and to complete a domain they must complete each competency. The objectives are the building blocks to which all WGU assessments are aligned. A domain, effectively a set of courses, is defined by WGU as a "cohesive organizational structure of a set of knowledge the activities, behaviors, experiences, attitudes, and values that pertain to the set" (Staker, quoting WGU).

For example, associated with an education degree are fourteen domains, which closely resemble a typical course, i.e. Foundations of Teaching, Natural Science, Early Childhood Education. Domains vary in their number of competencies from five to thirty-seven, and individual objectives for each competency vary from 27 to 341 (Staker, 2012). In the domain entitled College-Level Reasoning and Problem Solving, one competency requires that students gather and consider multiple perspectives and use them to generate multiple solutions to the problem. Two example objectives associated with this competency are "choose relevant information from multiple sources for evaluating a given problem" and "choose a variety of types of information pertaining to a given problem" (Staker, 2012).

The assessments are divided into two categories. Students first take a knowledge test, multiple-choice or some variant thereupon, to demonstrate their knowledge of key terms and concepts associated with the competency. These tests are administered and assessed via automated software in the WGU Learning Management System, the LMS. Many bare-bones educational programs, online or otherwise, might just stop at the multiple-choice test before awarding credits, but to its credit, WGU also requires students, after passing the knowledge test, to complete a "performance assessment" such as an essay, though many in the performance assessment field would challenge whether a short essay genuinely represents the level of performance including transfer that performance assessment usually entails. These "performance assessments" are graded by a member of the dedicated assessment team, a group of full-time graders who neither design nor deliver any instruction, but exclusively perform grading using a standard rubric for each competency. Grading is entirely pass-fail, with the logic that competency is, simply, binary: either one has demonstrated competency or one has not, and beyond that there is no significant differentiation. As is often said about competency-based learning, you wouldn't want an airline pilot or a neurosurgeon who passed their coursework with a C–; what you want to know is whether or not they are competent in their craft. (Staker, 2012)

Is WGU succeeding as an educational institution? Its graduates appear to think so, if we can trust the findings of a WGU-commissioned but independently researched report by the Gallup organization. Recent WGU alumni were surveyed and the results were compared to a large national sampling of alumni from colleges of all types and sizes: 83% of WGU alumni report holding full-time employment, compared to 64% of national; 72% report having full-time work related to their major in university compared to 39% of national; 72% report their college education was worth the cost compared to 37% of national; and 74% are extremely likely to recommend WGU to others, compared to 44% of national (The University of You, n.d.). WGU is accredited by the Northwest Commission on Colleges and Universities. But beyond accreditation and surveys, there is, as is noted in Connell (2011), a shortage of hard evidence. WGU is not alone in this shortage; Connell quotes David Longanecker, President of the Western Interstate Commission for Higher Education, as believing that that the entire online university sector lacks hard evidence, but that "WGU is doing as much as anyone else is" (Connell, 2011).

Johann Neem, a Washington state college professor, appreciates that some WGU students and alumni might indeed achieve their specific career goals, but states bluntly that WGU "does not offer a college education" (Neem, 2012).

Aspects of Neem's critique are, while important and penetrating, outside the scope of this inquiry about the lessons of this model for K-12 (kindergarten to grade 12) education, such as whether WGU deservedly met accreditation standards having to do with depth of faculty scholarship and range of faculty academic freedom. But other elements of his argument are critical for K-12 educators to reckon with. Neem begins with a philosophical unpacking of what a course of education really ought to be at its base. Is the demonstration of proficiency in knowledge and skills more important for success than the lived experience of deliberately and gradually developing that proficiency? Is education at base the destination or the journey? We must concern ourselves with whether the WGU model and competency-based crediting ultimately compromises or sacrifices altogether the journey for the destination. If you arrive at the top of Mount Everest by Star Trek-like "beaming," can you genuinely claim to have summited the world's tallest peak? And if learning has been so hurried, you'd want to check whether that peak on which you are standing is anything more than a mirage.

Neem also uses a learning-to-drive metaphor to explore competency-based education. Advocates for performance task assessment in lieu of multiple-choice and short-answer testing often point out that earning a driver's license requires passing a multiple-choice test and also demands successful completion of a road test—"performing" the competency for which one is being certified or credited. (Even better than a typical road test, we should say, would be one that demands test-takers drive on complicated routes and in challenging weather that they have previously not experienced.)

Neem writes, "We all know what it takes to pass a driving test, and we all know how to do it: we cram a bunch of stuff into short-term memory, and then pass a competency-based exam" (Neem, 2012). Neem clearly is referring here to the writing part of the test, because nobody would think you can just "cram stuff into memory" to pass the road driving test. But in doing so, he mistakes the meaning of competency-based exam; he is correct of course that driving license aspirants do exactly this cramming to prepare for and pass the written part of the driving test, but that is only half the process, and few if any educators who work in competency-based education would call the written test the Department of Motor Vehicles requires "competency-based."

Neem elaborates, "We know that becoming a driver is a much different process; it requires guidance and repeated practice (or seat time). WGU's approach might help students pass licensing exams, but it does not help them become drivers" (Neem, 2012). Again, he is correct that becoming a skilled driver and passing the driving test usually requires guidance and practice, but we cannot assume that a competency-based crediting approach like WGU's puts unprepared drivers on the road.

WGU requires neither repeated practice nor "seat time," but it does demand, at least in design and intent, that students pass the equivalent of a road test in a performance assessment, though as noted, a short essay is probably a poor example of such a performance. No aspiring driver is likely to be able to do so without the development through practice and guidance of those skills. But some suburban teenagers need this preparation by registering in a driver's ed class; some rural youth have been driving tractors for years; why require the same training for both?

Nevertheless, Neem's larger point is well taken. Learning can't be contained entirely in the assessment of learning. A degree or diploma that can be earned exclusively by completing end-of-term or competency-aligned assessments will represent an incomplete education, one undeserving of that degree or diploma. "Although commentators embrace WGU's model because it offers easily assessable outcomes, this may also be its problem" (Neem, 2012). Core learning, he writes, takes place "in the interactions between teachers and students, and between students themselves—the stuff that happens beyond the textbook" (Neem, 2012).

Those advocating for and implementing a WGU-type model of crediting for competencies, detached from required coursework, need to grapple with Neem's call for continued attention to the extended deliberative process of learning: the discussion and discovery, the dissonance and disequilibrium, the detours and dead ends that all ultimately ensure meaningful and lasting student learning.

Ultimately, while a useful case study in the form of a competency-based crediting system, WGU is as much a cautionary tale of the potential flaws or limitations of this approach as it is a model to learn from.

Lerner Medical College

Next up is the trailblazing innovation of Case Western Reserve University's Lerner Medical College (CCLCM), situated at the globally renowned hospital the Cleveland Clinic and founded just after the turn of this century. Lerner's leadership recognized that successful doctors must develop and demonstrate mastery of key competencies, not simply pass exams by displaying expertise in subject knowledge. Lerner has put this recognition into thorough practice through its competency-based assessment and digital, or ePortfolio, system.

Lerner describes itself as a "unique medical school program that sets standards for the training of physician investigators through innovative approaches to the integration of basic science, research and clinical medicine." The curriculum is fully problem-based, putting small groups to work on collaborative case-based analyses (Cleveland Clinic Lerner College of Medicine, n.d.).

Mastery Transcript Consortium founder Scott Looney views the Lerner competency-based assessment system as an influence on what the MTC aspires to do for secondary education (Looney, 2016). Looney's school, Hawken, is in Cleveland, and in the first-ever meeting of the MTC, in April 2016, Looney led the fifty attending educators on a field trip of sorts to the nearby Cleveland Clinic for a deep dive into Lerner's model, presented by Neil Mehta, Lerner's Assistant Dean (Mehta, 2016).

In a slide teeing up his explanation of Lerner's grading and crediting system, Dr. Mehta wrote: "No Grades, No Class Ranks!" To further detail, he explained its elements, defined by its:

- Learning portfolio—assessment of for learning
- No grades
- No high-stakes tests
- No class ranking

(Mehta, 2016)

At the foundation of the system are nine competencies that establish the breadth of demands placed upon the modern physician and medical researcher. No student and no professor in the program is ever unclear or unsure about what the nine competencies are. K-12 educators thinking about how to frame a competency-based secondary program would do well to look closely at the Lerner model, and the way it combines core academic, twenty-first-century skills, nonacademic, and reflection-synthesis competencies (Dannefer & Henson, 2007).

Competencies for Which Students Are Assessed at the Cleveland Clinic Lerner College of Medicine

1. Research

   Demonstrate knowledge base and critical-thinking skills for basic and clinical research and skill sets required to conceptualize and conduct research, and understand the ethical, legal, professional, and social issues required for responsible conduct of research

2. Basic and Clinical Sciences of Medical Knowledge

   Demonstrate and apply knowledge of human structure and function, pathophysiology, human development, and psychosocial concepts to medical practice

3. Communication

   Demonstrate effective verbal, nonverbal, and written communication skills in a wide range of relevant activities in medicine and research

4. Clinical Skills

   Perform appropriate history and physical examination in a variety of patient care encounters, and demonstrate effective use of clinical procedures and laboratory tests

5. Clinical Reasoning

   Diagnose, manage, and prevent common health problems of individuals, families, and communities. Interpret findings and formulate action plan to characterize the problem and reach a diagnosis

6. Professionalism

   Demonstrate knowledge and behavior that represents the highest standard of medical research and clinical practice, including compassion, humanism, and ethical and responsible actions at all times

7. Personal Development

   Recognize and analyze personal needs (learning, self-care, etc.), and implement plan for personal growth

8. Health Care Systems
   Recognize and be able to work effectively in the various health care systems to advocate and provide quality patient care
9. Reflective Practice
   Demonstrate habits of analyzing cognitive and affective experiences that result in identification of learning needs, leading to integration and synthesis of new learning.
   (Dannefer & Henson, 2007)

Numbers one through five together with eight represent the skills fundamental to the physician-researcher. Six and seven represent a far more holistic approach to medical education—highlighting personal attributes in a way that should be replicated in K-12 schooling competencies. Secondary educators, too, can hold them accountable for developing and displaying skills such as work ethic, respect and responsibility, self-direction, and personal growth.

Competency nine, meanwhile, was added because of concerns that a competency-based system can devolve into one where discrete skills are valued more than holistic and synthesized capabilities. This is particularly pertinent in the wake of the potential limitations of the WGU system identified above. As a medical journal article explains:

> Competency-based assessment has the potential to fragment performance by using methods that target specific components of competencies, thereby neglecting the complexity and integrated nature of practice. Thus, reflective practice is the foundational competency for the CCLCM program, underscoring the critical importance of learning from experience and engaging in conversations about practice to develop professional judgment.
>
> (Dannefer & Henson, 2007)

Here is an effective answer to Neem's critique of WGU; we need to ensure for greater intellectual development and lasting learning, we demand interactive deliberation and extended reflection.

As WGU works from domains to competencies to objectives and builds assessments for the objectives, Lerner works from competencies to standards: the "specific desired outcomes" for each competency. These standards are developmentally differentiated, set for years one, two, and five (the final year), but "because the CCLCM curriculum is individualized during years three through five, students can potentially meet year five standards at variable time points" (Dannefer & Henson, 2007). This is an important facet to the program and the larger model. Most competency-based crediting systems aspire to avoid restrictions by year or time.

Here is an example of the year five standards for a communication competency:

- Uses effective written and oral communication when interacting in formal and informal settings with a wide variety of individuals and groups.
- Practices effective patient-centered communication under all circumstances.
- Demonstrates coherent, concise, and grammatically correct written communication.
- Demonstrates ability to reflect on and appropriately modify responses while interacting with others.

(Dannefer & Henson, 2007)

Defining objectives or standards is not even half the battle. At WGU, a simple two-part system was implemented to assess students against each of the objectives: a knowledge check and a performance task. Examples of evidence of performance include "oral presentations, research proposals, problem-solving essays, observed history and physicals, patient logs, NBME [National Board of Medical Examiners] progress tests" (Dannefer & Henson, 2007). Note that these appear to be considerably more robust tasks than the short essays WGU defines as performances.

At Lerner, time was taken to thoroughly develop a comprehensive and almost idealistic vision of an assessment philosophy before tackling the nuts and bolts. After careful and thorough research in assessment practices (a process all schools embarking on this work should undertake), the faculty arrived at a set of key design principles, among them:

- The goal of assessment is to enhance student learning.
- Assessment will be progressive and cumulative to encourage integration of previous material with new knowledge and to assess mastery of prior areas of weakness.

- Ongoing cycles of self-assessment and advisement from faculty will ensure that students master areas of relative weakness and develop further in areas of relative strength.

(Dannefer & Henson, 2007)

This represents an effort to balance formative and summative assessment, and to implement a system of continuous improvement for student learning and the assessment system itself. K-12 educators would be similarly advised to pause before building their competency credit system so they can review and determine their own assessment philosophy and guiding principles, and then design their system to match.

Working from those design principles, the faculty at Lerner created an e-portfolio assessment system, one that the educators there are determined to perpetuate and improve. This aspect of the Lerner system appears to have been especially influential upon the founders and planners of the Mastery Transcript Consortium. As the article notes, the e-portfolio system was selected only after a rigorous review of various options and systems, and was selected because it could best "promote reflection on learning, accommodate a wide range of assessments, including authentic performance-based methods, and give students responsibility for integrating and assessing evidence of their own learning" (Dannefer & Henson, 2007).

Lerner's system is an elaborate system with many moving parts, but it is worth unpacking the many ways in which it can guide the work of K-12 educators. Central to its structure is its bimodality, containing both a large formative assessment component and also a thorough summative one. The formative portfolios (FPs) and summative portfolios (SPs) are contained within the same system, built on the same competencies and assessed against the same standards, and employ the same expansive pool of evidence—but are also entirely separate channels, such that the summative assessment review has no access to or input from the formative area. As the article explains, this will "ensure that confidentiality of reflections of a personal nature is not compromised by the rigor and judgments required for making promotion decisions" (Dannefer & Henson, 2007).

At the base of this system is the evidence database, containing what might become hundreds, even thousands, of individual units of data: lab reports, journals, short assessments from supervisors, peer assessments, patient logs, etc. As Dr. Mehta explains, the system must be highly flexible to allow an effectively infinite range of items to be entered, contained, and searched. Over time, participants realized the critical importance of tagging evidence to the nine competencies to greatly ease the organizational structure. "Student responsibility for selecting evidence and analysis of their learning is critical to maintaining student engagement in assessing progress" (Dannefer & Henson, 2007).

The collection of the evidence is essential, but the reflection upon the evidence is where the system becomes most complete. In both the FP (formative) and SP (summative) procedures, the students reviews their evidence and write essays reflecting upon their growth in (FP) and demonstrating their achievement of (SP) each of the nine competencies, citing, of course, extensive evidence to support their claims. The FP reflections are also accompanied by student-prepared future learning plans—including measurable outcomes and reviews of previous plans (Dannefer & Henson, 2007).

The FP reviews are conducted by the student's adviser, who evaluates the student's effectiveness in addressing the patterns of performance the evidence establishes, the student's quality of reflection, and the strength of the improvement plan. The SP reflections, which the student completes at the end of years one, two, and five, are first reviewed by the adviser to ensure that the work is the student's own and that the evidence accurately reflects the breadth of the data collected. It is then reviewed by a panel composed of fifteen thoroughly trained faculty members (Dannefer & Henson, 2007).

The committee does not jump directly to reviewing the portfolio reflections; it instead first works together on a set of eight randomly selected submissions to conduct a thorough standard-setting process, including individual and group review and rating, in order to enhance inter-rater reliability. Only thereafter are the remainder of the submissions reviewed by committee members in pairs, who must agree on their rating or bring it to the full committee. There are only three determinations for each student: met, not met, or provided insufficient evidence for the standard; there are no grades. At the end of the review, "Every student receives a letter that summarizes the outcome of the committee's deliberations and that notes specific strengths and areas needing improvement" (Dannefer & Henson, 2007).

As the authors of the article note in the discussion of key design elements:

Rigorous measurement standards are necessary if portfolios are to be used for summative purposes: fairness (clear instructions, equal assistance, and due process), validity (appropriate standards, evaluators capable of making sound judgments, and quality authentic evidence), and reliability (trained evaluators and adequate curricular experiences providing multiple sources of assessment).

(Dannefer & Henson, 2007)

Note the emphasis here on a very high threshold for credits being awarded; this is a Pass-Fail system, it would appear, where the passing definition is set at an A, not a C. The competency-based crediting systems that will be most successful, and most lasting, will have similarly high bars.

One Lerner graduate explained in a presentation that having such an alternative transcript might surprise some hiring committees, which caused anxiety. He explained, as quoted in Grant Lichtman's book *Moving the Rock*:

In a given year, we probably get more than 150 individual items of feedback from our teachers and peers on our performance and we reflect on many of those. So I walked into the interview with this huge stack of paper, which was the only real evidence I had of my work during the past five years. As soon as the interview started, one of the doctors interviewing me asked what the stack was, and I explained it to him. He says, "so let me get this right: for five years, every day and every week, you are getting review and feedback from teachers and peers that is directly related to your learning and practice in medicine?" I nodded, yes. He said "the interview is over; you are accepted."

(Lichtman, 2017)

Admittedly the story has an apocryphal ring to it; moreover, there is no good excuse for not providing a student emerging from such a competency-based crediting system a concise and clearly communicated transcript of accomplishments. (Nor is it clear why an e-portfolio would have left this student with "a huge stack of paper.") But the story does reveal the value of a system so thoroughly built to enhance formative assessment and to give credit for demonstrated skills, not simply course completion.

Helpfully, the Dannefer and Henson journal article concludes with a series of recommendations for effective portfolio assessment. Although the dozen-odd suggestions are intended for other medical colleges, many of them are nonetheless very appropriate to K-12 educators developing similar models. From the article's twelve tips, three key themes emerge.

First among them is giving due attention to the quality and quantity of the evidence entered into the portfolio. The authors write that "We learned very quickly that faculty and students need to be trained to provide observation-based, narrative feedback on the performance-based criteria to identify areas needing improvement and areas of strength" (Dannefer & Henson, 2017). This requires rigorous training for faculty, and also guidance to students on how to provide and receive quality feedback from peers. It's also critical that students be provided with the experiences and opportunities necessary for them to collect supporting evidence in each competency. "If a review by the curriculum committees finds that curricular experiences and/or opportunities to obtain quality feedback are insufficient to demonstrate achievement of standards, standards are revised or the educational program (curriculum, assessments, etc.) is improved" (Dannefer & Henson, 2017).

Second is the importance of carefully cultivating a culture of assessment quality amongst the faculty. For most professors of medicine, as for many secondary teachers, competency-based assessment is not intuitive. This is not an educational approach that they themselves experienced as students, and a significant shift is required. At Lerner, this entailed developing multiple channels of communication, including letters and reminders, extensive training, and a full-blown faculty conference (Dannefer & Henson, 2017).

Third, quality and improvement is best supported by an oversight committee dedicated to the assessment process, which "ensures its integrity by establishing policies consistent with the assessment principles" (Dannefer & Henson, 2017). This committee ought to appoint or annoint experts in the portfolio system as a whole or in specific competency areas. To manage the system's continuous improvement, the committee should systematize a through process of collecting feedback by all participants. It is also vital for this oversight group to maintain close attention to ensuring validity and reliability in assessment through thorough review and analysis of the process and outcomes.

As far removed as medical college may seem from high school, Lerner's trailblazing work offers excellent modeling and valuable insights for the work of transforming secondary education to competency-based assessment, crediting, and diplomas.

New Zealand's National Certificate of Educational Achievement (NCEA)

Where might we find a useful example of competency-based crediting in a secondary school context? Is this really doable in high school? Fortunately, there is a program with a near fifteen-year history in a nation not too terribly unlike the US.

Secondary education in New Zealand experienced a massive shift almost fifteen years ago when the nation's education ministry adopted the National Certificate of Educational Achievement (NCEA). It is the main qualification for secondary school students in NZ: in effect a high school diploma, the only high school diploma, available for Kiwi students. NCEA is administered by the NZQA, the New Zealand Qualifications Authority, a government entity tasked with providing leadership in assessment and qualifications (National Certificate of Educational Achievement (NCEA), n.d.).

NCEA is thoroughly described in various governmental documents, and has been written about from the educator perspective widely on various blogs and other platforms in New Zealand. It is also discussed in a recent book by an NZ school administrator, Richard Wells, entitled *A Learner's Paradise: How New Zealand is Reimagining Education*. I had the opportunity to visit New Zealand in 2017 and visit educators in four secondary schools there. At each school, I observed classes, interviewed students and teachers, and acquired a first-hand impression of the interesting, impressive, and highly differentiated NCEA system.

NCEA operates, in a sense, in two dimensions: in one dimension, as practiced in a high proportion (90%, one NZ educator estimated) of high schools, the innovative model has been corralled and configured into traditional modes of teaching, learning, and assessing. Though the bottles may be new, the wine is old: little has been genuinely transformed. This is a caution and a caveat to US and global educators seeking to transform secondary schooling through the vehicle of an alternative transcript. But in a second dimension, powerful transformation is occurring, made available by the flexibility that NCEA affords and inspires.

NCEA academic subjects are divided into standards: literally, "thousands of purposefully open-ended competency and knowledge topic standards" defining what students need to know and show they can do (Wells, 2016).

Some example English written language standards from Level 2:

- Analyse specified aspect(s) of studied written text(s), supported by evidence
- Analyse significant aspects of unfamiliar written text(s) through close reading, supported by evidence
- Produce a selection of crafted and controlled writing
- Analyse significant connections across texts, supported by evidence
- Use information literacy skills to form developed conclusion(s)

(NCEA Standards, n.d.)

And some example Level 2 Science standards:

- Carry out quantitative analysis
- Carry out procedures to identify ions present in solution
- Demonstrate understanding of the chemistry used in the development of a current technology
- Demonstrate understanding of bonding, structure, properties and energy changes

(NCEA Standards, n.d.)

Each standard is worth some small number of credits, usually between three and six, that students earn and accumulate toward gaining a certificate at Levels 1, 2, and 3. Transcripts list the credits they've earned for each standard achieved. Different NCEA levels achieved establish student qualifications for career and/or "uni" (i.e. post-secondary) tracks: Level 2, for instance, might suit some employers just fine; universities typically demand Level 3. Attaining each level requires earning eighty credits. In Level 1, ten of the eighty must be in literacy (writing, speaking and listening skills) and ten must be in numeracy (number, measurement and statistical skills). Even these specific baseline credits can be earned in any number of ways, and they can't be earned simply by completing seat time in a course labeled literacy or numeracy. Standards and credits are defined and tied to a specific level; achieving a Level 1 certificate requires earning eighty Level 1 or higher credits; achieving a Level 2 requires earning sixty Level 2 or higher credits, and twenty credits from any of the three levels; and likewise, achieving Level 3 requires earning sixty Level 3 credits and twenty credits from Level 2 or Level 3 (How NCEA Works, n.d.).

Most students begin their NCEA levels with Level 1 work in what NZ calls Year 11 (tenth grade equivalent in the US), going on to Level 2 in Year 12 (eleventh grade), and Level 3 in Year 13 (twelfth grade). But there's plenty of mixing and matching, and students can move at their own speed with no limitation to faster or slower paces as defined by the NCEA system (though there may be constraints within their particular schools). Students can even find themselves in a specific course (say, Year 11 English) that addresses standards at both Level 1 and Level 2 (How NCEA Works, n.d.).

As explained by NZQA, "Credits may be accumulated from different learning institutions or workplaces towards a single qualification. All organisations with consent to assess against standards recognise credits awarded by others." Standards come in two flavors: unit standards, which are defined by industry councils and special qualification units, and achievement standards, defined by NZQA (How NCEA Works, n.d.).

What about assessment of students meeting standards, and the consequential awarding of credits? This happens in two ways: external assessments, via national exams or portfolio submission to a national agency panel, or internal assessments. Many students earn their credits for NCEA standards through national exams, called external assessments, administered by NZQA. These national exams, or portfolio submissions, are very loosely analogous to Advanced Placement (AP) or International Baccalaureate (IB) exams in the US.

Internal assessments open the door to much more innovative and interdisciplinary learning. Wells provides examples of teachers and students leveraging NCEA this way, evaluated and credited by "internal assessments." In one example:

> Teachers began to design projects that encapsulated two or more standards in larger pieces of work. Learning areas such as technology were able to switch from assessing isolated skill competencies

(such as making a webpage or robot) to large, product-development projects issuing credits for developing briefs and analysing markets and stakeholders for their technology products.

(Wells, 2016)

In another:

One teacher whose school was alongside the beach created a sustainability project based around surfboard product development, where students had to build fully recyclable boards that catered to specific surfers' performance needs as well as their rather fussy design preferences. This project utilised five NCEA Standards, earning students a quarter of their year's requirements in credits.

(Wells, 2016)

All assessments are graded, not with letter grades but with four tiers: not achieved, achieved, merit, and excellence. The system, as different as it seems on its face, functions in a way that often allows nonetheless for traditional courses of study and traditional methods of awarding, in effect, the rough equivalent of letter grades. Take a course, take a national exam, be graded and awarded credits: nothing exciting or transformative here to see (How NCEA Works, n.d.).

However, as rigidly implemented and experienced as the system often is, it also allows for a much greater range of innovation in the following ways.

1. Students can earn their eighty credits by drawing from an extraordinarily wide array of standards (in addition to the required literacy and numeracy credits in level one, which amount in total to a quarter of that level and a twelfth of the entirety of the three levels.) Students can choose hereby to craft far greater unique or individualized learning pathways and experiences.

2. Students can learn the content and skills they need to achieve any standard entirely on their own or via courses of study outside formal schooling, take the national exam to earn the credits, and still achieve the various certificates. No standard is necessarily tied to any specific course, and accordingly, no specific class or Carnegie-style credits (such as Algebra 1, US History, Biology, or English 1) is in any way obligatory.

3. Internal assessments open the door to much greater flexibility, and ultimately, greater transformative opportunity. Internal assessments are used to assess skills and knowledge that cannot be tested in an exam or placed in a formal. Internal assessments make it possible for students to forgo all or nearly all external exams, and earn their credits through internal assessments and portfolio submission. (Quality concerns about this alternative pathway are assuaged by knowing that the NZQA monitors internal assessment and portfolio assessment in an annual review of a randomly selected sampling to ensure consistency and quality, a process called moderation.)

4. Because these credits can be mixed and matched, they can be organized into an infinite array of transdisciplinary course options, authentic experiences in the workforce or service, or personalized learning journeys. As Wells explains:

> The open-ended design of these standards is meant to allow teachers and, more recently, students to devise projects and work that would best show excellence-level thinking and understanding. Teachers and students can develop projects using collections of standards from different disciplines. This way, an authentic project with the power to make real change in a community could be devised. For example, a project's demand for communication, scientific experiment, product design, marketing, and evaluation could all be assessed by the relevant standards and possibly offer a student around half his or her qualification needs for the year.
>
> (Wells, 2016)

Successful exploitation of the opportunity NCEA offers can be found in several impressive school programs in New Zealand. One of the most prominent examples is that of Hobsonville Point Secondary School (HPSS), situated in a recently developed area on the outskirts of Auckland. The school makes for a breathtaking visit from the first steps on campus. A long passageway runs the length of the building, adjacent to a series of laboratories, design labs, makerspaces, flexible seating arrangements, nooks and carrels, and even dedicated spaces for startup technology companies hosted in glass-walled office spaces amidst student learning labs: entrepreneurial and scientific professionals working right alongside and intermingling with secondary students and teachers.

; the school, one encounters students working in a wide variety
ı a few open spaces, students sit in desks in rows, the class led by
ut more often, students work in small groups, conducting experi-
igning and prototyping, and making plans for internships with
advisers. Upon inquiry, nearly every student could speak specifically to the
standards they were working to master for credits and to the progress of their
individual or small group journeys toward completion. American educational
expert Grant Lichtman noticed in his visit that "Students clearly understand
and can articulate why they are learning, how it applies to the world around
them, and why the learning will help them in the future" (Lichtman, 2015).

That students and teachers can work toward achieving credits
untethered to particular courses means that the schedule is designed far
more flexibly.

> The daily schedule is unlike any other I have seen, with time for
> instruction, community planning, passion-based units, social time,
> and the other elements of a balanced, deeper learning experience.
> Content and subjects are included within broad multi-teacher inter-
> disciplinary programs.
>
> (Lichtman, 2015)

Richard Wells similarly writes of the HPSS schedule:

> Every time slot on the timetable is dedicated to student-driven and
> designed projects and reflection. For the projects, issues and topics
> are brought up for consideration by students and teachers. From
> those topics, students plan, either in groups or independently,
> how to best tackle the projects and how to ensure the learning
> process leads to real outcomes. The result of these projects is that
> the school is having quite an impact on the local community.
>
> (Wells, 2016)

Visible throughout those long halls are vivid and expansive displays
of broad student project work. As the school website explains, and as the
NCEA's flexibility makes possible:

> Learning projects are a key curriculum element at Hobsonville Point
> and are an important way of students learning in and beyond the

school environment. Learners are engaged in at least one short or long term project at any time. There are two strands to learning projects: school-wide "Big Projects" and "Passion Projects".

Big Projects (Year 9–10) are ongoing, longer term projects facilitated by the school [using] partnerships with external businesses and groups, [providing] scope for student participation across a wide range of roles; [these] include a philanthropy/service element, and potential projects link to cross-curriculum themes: sustainability, wetlands, ethical clothing, musical production, sports academy, makerspace/robotics.

Impact Projects (Year 11–12) include individual/team negotiated projects initiated from student interest, and link with internal &/or external expertise, mentoring, placement.

(HPSS—Project Learning, n.d.)

At HPSS, students craft personalized learning pathways aided by a personal "Learning Coach" from the faculty. Together, they identify interests and passions, set challenging goals, and work to ensure that their individual learning is relevant to them. Sometimes this means they tackle specifically selected standards matched to their interests and aspirations; sometimes it means they choose particular learning modules that meet their needs. Modules are cross-curricular experiences taught by teams of teachers and provide:

the depth and breadth of curriculum and wider conceptual coverage. This gives students a choice of connection and context eg a Maths with Physical Education co-module, or English and Science. All modules are delivered by specialist teachers at the appropriate curriculum levels and build on a wider Big Concept each term eg Space & Place or Identity.

(HPSS—Specialised Learning, n.d.)

As the school's principal Maurie Abrams explains, "We are doing this because we are committed to bringing life to the potential of the NCEA and to make secondary schooling more relevant for young people" (Wells, 2016).

Kia Aroha College provides another example of a school effectively creating a unique and personally relevant curriculum under the NCEA model. It would be hard for Kia Aroha to be any more different from HPSS in student demographics; it is a secondary school located on the other side of Auckland, in one of its lowest income neighborhoods, designed to educate Maori and Pasifika students. According to its principal, it features a "learning approach that encourages the development of our students' cultural identity and home languages, in two distinct 'schools' within the campus—Te Whānau o Tupuranga (Centre for Māori Education) and Fanau Pasifika (Centre for Pasifika Education)" (Nau Mai, n.d.).

Because Kia Aroha isn't constrained by organizing learning around a specific set of required courses, it can provide its students and families a far more culturally responsive and personalized learning pathway. Its website makes this explicit: "In the Senior School we believe learning must be individually personalised to the learner, to their interests, strengths and career pathways. The following links show the possible selections and progression through each NCEA Level." Pedagogical philosophy is built on indigenous cultural values: "Whanau/Family and a pedagogy that develops relationships of trust and mutual respect is the 'glue' that CONNECTS everything together. A pedagogy of whanau includes support, community and leadership'" (Kia Aroha College, n.d.).

Although these two schools reflect vastly different cultures and perspectives, HPSS being futuristic in outlook and form, seeking to align itself with the fast-changing future of professional work, and Kia Aroha instead drawing deeply from ancient and relevant cultural traditions for its instructional design and values, they share some similar commitments— most of all, that education should be designed for student connection, engagement, and impact. As Kia Aroha's site states:

> Our model involves young people in participatory action research, in the study of issues and concerns that impact on their lives, families, and communities—and provides them with the tools to make change in the world. The curriculum is organised around problems and issues that are of personal and social significance in the real world.
>
> (Kia Aroha College, n.d.)

Sadly, these two schools are the exception, not the rule. Many educators in New Zealand feel stymied by school cultures unwilling to change and by communities discomforted by true transformation. NCEA allows for varying approaches yet is rarely leveraged for transformation. Claire Amos, an influential voice for progressive education in Auckland, explains it this way:

> [We keep hearing] the tried and true excuses for retaining the status quo. The community doesn't want fewer standards. Students love exams. Parents love exams. What about our Metro magazine results and league tables? We don't want to narrow the curriculum. Schools were still thinking in siloed subjects and somehow seeing exams as more valuable than internal assessment. So much value was placed on the perception of outsiders and assumptions about what the community, board, teachers and students think and feel. Student wellbeing and creativity was completely AWOL as drivers in any of the discussions I was privy to.
>
> (Amos, 2018)

Visiting the oldest high school in the nation's capital, Wellington High, I heard similar messages from a nationally recognized educational innovator who serves as a senior school administrator, who told me that little about the school's curriculum or instruction has changed because of NCEA. The course catalog is nearly indistinguishable from two decades ago: most teachers teach as they have always taught. NCEA might open windows for innovation, but there is no obligation for schools to climb through.

For Amos, "NCEA is already incredibly flexible and designed to be a veritable smorgasbord of standards that can be combined and curated, mixed and multi-levelled to respond to the strengths, interests and needs of our learners." The failing, in her eyes, is the leadership of schools. "The problem lies in the lack of design. Schools, for the most part, have been sleepwalking through NCEA" (Amos, 2018).

Wells similarly wrestles with the slow pace of change in New Zealand. He writes that it may require "massive effort and commitment," and cautions readers with the "hope that you'll take comfort in slow progress." Indeed, it "may take a decade or so before you see significant progress" (Wells, 2016).

It is not only the educational progressives who hold concerns about NCEA; those from the other side of the pedagogical spectrum are anxious, too. To them, NCEA is too unstructured and too permissive, and, as a result, compromises the fundamentals. In a 2018 report, revealingly titled *Spoiled by Choice*, author Briar Lipson claims that, in NCEA:

> Students can gain qualifications in specific skills or knowledge without needing to master whole subjects. The hope is that this way schooling becomes more child-centred, practical, relevant and engaging to the full spectrum of students. Such was NCEA's promise: but its flexibility has been bought at unquantified cost.
>
> (Lipson, 2018)

Lipson argues that, although student achievement as measured within the NCEA system has risen by its own barometer during its fifteen-year history, New Zealand's PISA and other international testing performance has suffered. Although it should be noted there are no certain causes for PISA performance change over time, she places the blame for decline on NCEA's minimal emphasis on required study of the basics, reading and math (literacy and numeracy): "CEA all but abandoned the idea of a core curriculum requirement" (Lipson, 2018).

As noted, it is only in Level 1 that NCEA has any requirements at all, and they represent only ten units of literacy and numeracy each, out of eighty; Lipson characterizes even these as "loosely defined." Beyond this small obligation, she says, "all subjects—from meat processing to mathematics—are valued equally. This means well-advised or motivated students can still achieve a broad and valuable education. However, for poorly-advised or less motivated students, NCEA also offers a plethora of 'safer' alternatives" (Lipson, 2018). US educators, including those supportive of the Mastery Transcript Consortium, should take Lipson's cautions to heart, and consider carefully whether the core learning requirements in MTC's model, and in other competency-based crediting models, for every student are substantial enough, whether their school's center can hold.

Lipson's other concern is the burden of increased assessment obligations on teachers, and the potential narrowing of the curriculum to only those standards that are easily assessed. In a conventional high school course that is recorded as completed with traditional Carnegie units on a typical transcript, students and teachers might go several weeks without administering and evaluating assessments, and they might spend several days on topics of interest—such as current events, or recent scientific findings—that have no assessments. This isn't to say this is well advised; more frequent formative assessment is strongly supported by research for greater learning outcomes. It is just to say that the shift to a vastly more frequent assessment load may be burdensome for teachers.

In NCEA, Lipson complains, the dissolution of courses into distinct standards, each assessed individually—what she calls "chunking"—results in considerably increased assessment volume and teacher workload. She also argues that teachers, working to ensure that students are ready to succeed on standards when being "internally assessed," often focus closely on NCEA sample assessments to inform internal assessment, replicating them year to year and teaching narrowly to them. As a result, a program intended to promote flexible and broader learning, to stimulate creativity and curiosity, unintentionally yields more teaching to the test (Lipson, 2018).

NCEA, as dramatic innovations often are, is barraged with concerns and complaints from many angles. As of summer 2018, the new government led by Jacinda Arden is making a substantial effort to reform the program and correct its flaws. New Education Minister Chris Hipkins is leading a charge to reinvigorate and bolster the NCEA framework with what he has labeled "The 6 Big Opportunities" (Hipkins, 2018).

These six ideas respond to both major waves of criticism: that of what we might call the educational left (that schools are still far too traditional in their practices) and that of the right (that students are not being effectively prepared with foundational knowledge and skills). This reform movement also seeks to address an area that is harder to categorize as right or left: the impact on teacher workload (Hipkins, 2018).

To address the criticism that most Level 1 students are assessed primarily by national exam, not internal assessment, Hipkins' first opportunity proposes halving Level 1 required units from eighty to forty, maintaining twenty for foundational literacy and numeracy and placing the other twenty into a required extended project. "Projects can be used to explore ideas and actions that make a difference in students' lives, while developing the knowledge, skills, and attitudes they need for the future" (Hipkins, 2018).

Another of the six ideas expands on this, exploring whether projects connected to work and the community should become a required part of NCEA Levels 2 and 3. This:

could include credits from a "pathways opportunity," such as a research or community project, progress towards an out-of-school qualification, industry training or a work placement. Many students enjoy learning opportunities that take them out of the classroom and let them explore the pathways they could take to work or tertiary study. At times, these opportunities can be undervalued by NCEA. Levels 2 and 3 could encourage these student-led opportunities and make sure they are clearly linked to NCEA.

(Hipkins, 2018)

Addressing other concerns is a "big opportunity" from Hipkins that addresses concerns of poor core academic skill preparation. It calls for a thorough review of all literacy and numeracy standards and credit assessments to provide greater assurance that students are prepared for future learning and demanding work. It also asks whether literacy and numeracy should be expanded to include concepts such as digital and financial savviness (Hipkins, 2018).

Another "opportunity" focuses on teachers and curricular innovation, aiming to reduce the assessment pressure on teachers. "Changes in resourcing and support, moderation expectations, quality assurance, and accountability could help make this vision easier. This would support teachers to lead these shifts from the ground up and strengthen teaching practice while reducing workload and stress." It also aims to revisit school schedules and other school features so as to enhance opportunities for the design of "courses that cater to student interests, passions, and needs and that emphasise, their most important ideas, knowledge, and skills" (Hipkins, 2018).

The last of the six "big opportunities" addresses transcripts specifically, or what are referred to in NZ as "records." Currently, these records document only the standards achieved and credits earned for those standards, "but it doesn't demonstrate a student's full knowledge, skills, attitudes, and capabilities." The proposed reforms call for opening the record of achievement to valuable information for both post-secondary (or "tertiary") institutions and employers that "acknowledges and values things like employment, community work, extracurricular activities and cultural contributions" (Hipkins, 2018).

Like Western Governors University and Lerner Medical College, the example of New Zealand's National Certificate of Education

Achievement provides US educators—and educators globally—a great deal of information to consider when developing and implementing a competency-based crediting system. US and other educators exploring or implementing similar crediting and transcript changes are advised to look to Wells's book, Lipson's *Spoiled by Choice* report, and Hipkins' Six Big Opportunities.

References

Amos, C. (2018, February 26). NCEA—We Need to Review Our Mindset First. Retrieved September 16, 2018, from https://teachingandelearning.blogspot.com/2018/02/ncea-we-need-to-review-our-mindset-first.html

Cleveland Clinic Lerner College of Medicine (n.d.). Retrieved September 16, 2018, from https://portals.clevelandclinic.org/cclcm/

Connell, C. (2011). *At No-Frills Western Governors University, the Path to a College Degree is Only as Long as Students Make It* (Report). New York, NY: Hechinger Institute on Education and the Media.

Dannefer, E. F. & Henson, L. C. (2007). The Portfolio Approach to Competency-Based Assessment at the Cleveland Clinic Lerner College of Medicine. *Academic Medicine, 82*(5), 493–502. doi:10.1097/acm.0b013e31803ead30

Hipkins, C. (2018). Big, Bold Ideas to Change NCEA—Do You Agree? Retrieved September 16, 2018, from www.beehive.govt.nz/release/big-bold-ideas-change-ncea-%E2%80%93-do-you-agree

How NCEA works (NCEA) (n.d.). Retrieved September 16, 2018, from www.nzqa.govt.nz/ncea/understanding-ncea/how-ncea-works

HPSS—Project Learning (n.d.). Retrieved September 16, 2018, from https://sites.google.com/hobsonvillepoint.school.nz/hpss/curriculum/project-learning

HPSS—Specialised Learning (n.d.). Retrieved September 16, 2018, from https://sites.google.com/hobsonvillepoint.school.nz/hpss/curriculum/specialised-learning

Kia Aroha College (n.d.). Retrieved September 16, 2018, from www.kiaaroha.school.nz/

Lichtman, G. (2015, October 16). High School of the Future? Retrieved September 16, 2018, from www.grantlichtman.com/high-school-of-the-future/

Lichtman, G. (2017). *Moving the Rock: Seven Levers We Can Press to Transform Education.* San Francisco, CA: Jossey-Bass.

Lipson, B. (2018). *Spoiled by Choice: How NCEA Hampers Education, and What it Needs to Succeed* (Report). Wellington, NZ: The New Zealand Initiative.

Looney, S. (2016, April 28). Mastery Transcript Consortium. Presentation presented at Mastery Transcript Consortium Meeting in Cleveland Botanical Garden, Cleveland, Ohio.

Mehta, N. (2016, April 28). *A Unique Medical School Program.* Lecture presented at Mastery Transcript Consortium Meeting, Cleveland, Ohio.

National Certificate of Educational Achievement (n.d.). Retrieved September 16, 2018, from www.nzqa.govt.nz/ncea/

Nau Mai (n.d.). Retrieved September 16, 2018, from www.kiaaroha.school.nz/nau-mai/

NCEA Standards. (n.d.). Retrieved September 16, 2018, from www.nzqa.govt.nz/qualifications-standards/standards/

Neem, J. (2012). A University Without Intellectuals: Western Governors University and the Academy's Future. *Thought & Action*, 28, 63–79.

The University of You (n.d.). Retrieved September 16, 2018, from www.wgu.edu/about/students-graduates.html#close

Wells, R. (2016). *A Learner's Paradise: How New Zealand is Reimagining Education*. Irvine, CA: EdTechTeam Press.

Western Governors University (2018, August 20). Retrieved September 16, 2018, from www.wgu.edu/

3

The Mastery Transcript Consortium

Here we look at the origin and development of a recent prominent example of competency-based crediting, that of the Mastery Transcript Consortium (MTC). The MTC, both organization and transcript, is a work in progress, fast-evolving and changing year to year. By the time the reader reads this book, its components may well have evolved considerably from its design at the time of this writing. The MTC transcript was proposed and described in an initial form during a series of meetings in 2016 and 2017, many of which this author participated in and contributed to (see the Acknowledgments for more information on this). This book treats the 2016 to 2018 MTC transcript vision and description as a valuable model of what competency-based crediting (CBC) might look like and could accomplish.

Scott Looney, Head of the Hawken School in Cleveland, had served schools long enough and observed closely enough to know that high school students were hurting and that curriculum innovation was being stifled: something needed to be done. In April 2016, he hosted a meeting of sixty-odd educators and school leaders to kick off a project that he and some colleagues, including Assistant Head of School Doris Korda, had been discussing for some time and in recent months had begun sharing with a widening circle of associates across the United States. Twenty-nine independent (private) schools were represented in a meeting room of the Cleveland Botanical Garden, along with a about a dozen other educational writers and consultants, this author included. The project: to create a new kind of high school transcript.

The event was partially financed by Ted Dintersmith, a former venture capitalist who has made educational transformation his new occupation, and who was the producer of the popular documentary film *Most Likely to Succeed.* In his 2018 book, *What School Could Be: Insights and Inspirations from Teachers Across America,* Dintersmith explains his reasoning for supporting a new transcript: "Change the high school transcript, and you change high school" (Dintersmith, 2018).

Looney cited Buckminster Fuller in his opening slide—"You never change things by fighting the existing reality. To change something, build a new model that makes the existing model obsolete"—before recounting his school's journey to this moment. The aim, he began, was to generate more authentic student learning in his mostly traditional college preparatory school. While others use terms like twenty-first-century, deeper, progressive, or personalized learning, Looney characterizes his vision with the metaphor of an "apprenticeship." The apprenticeship model, he said, serves these purposes and represents these qualities:

- Connects learning to the Real World
- Individualizes pace of learning
- Individualizes approach of learning
- Is "MASTERY" based not "TIME" based
- Creates incremental success, not winners and losers
- Exposes students to complexity
- Is ACTIVE learning, not PASSIVE
- Positions adults as coaches, not judges

(Looney, 2016)

Looney shared a highlight of his school's work to provide an "apprenticeship"-like curriculum: an interdisciplinary, multi-course-credit, the entrepreneurship semester course, with these descriptors:

- About startups
- Real problem-based learning
- Team-based learning
- Intrinsically interdisciplinary
- Making strategic use of community resources
- Highly experiential, collaborative, dynamic

(Looney, 2016)

Looney then identified the "boulders" that stood in the way of the "apprenticeship" schooling vision. One was time and the daily and weekly school schedule, which his team shifted to better support the apprenticeship model. The school needed different kinds of meeting spaces and a location more proximate to downtown businesses and organizations, and this "boulder" was moved with the purchase and renovation of a building close to internship opportunities (Looney, 2016).

But the next boulder proved more challenging: adequately representing this new course on a conventional high school transcript. He and his team found it simply couldn't do the new program justice. Indeed, in some cases, this exciting new course couldn't be recognized very well at all by the transcript norms, expectations, even requirements, of colleges, universities, and other institutions such as the NCAA (National College Athletic Association). He explained the problem this way:

> Our transcripts are products of industrial-era thinking in a digital age. Current transcripts privilege and promote:
>
> - Single Credit, Discipline Based Courses
> - Short Block Teaching
> - De-contextualized learning
> - Letter Grades
> - Time based (snapshot) Assessment
>
> (Looney, 2016)

Instead, he and Korda came to recognize that they needed a formal and shareable record of student achievement that could effectively convey the learning of the entrepreneurship semester program, impress post-secondary readers, and display the skills and competencies these students were developing and demonstrating. They also realized that, in contrast to the other boulders, this boulder could not be moved individually. College admission departments didn't want to learn to read and interpret a one-off outlier transcript. But with many allies on their side, Hawken's team believed they could leverage the numbers to bring college admissions to accept an alternative (Looney, 2016).

It was from this sequence of events that Looney confronted the limiting force, the nineteenth-century vestigial organ, that is the transcript. In both the presentation in Cleveland in April 2016 and on the MTC website, he lays out the case that the conventional transcript is both a broken tool and an absurdity. "The high school transcript aims to assess student progress and performance, but it is a broken instrument that underserves students, teachers or the world outside our school walls" (Mastery Transcript Consortium, n.d.).

How so? Because, as the MTC website elaborates:

- It focuses on the acquisition of information than the making of meaning.
- It is a remnant of the industrial age and takes its cues from the meatpacking industry.
- It pretends that a grade issued by an individual teacher is replicated, validated, and meaningful.
- It ignores noncognitive skills, also known a character traits.
- It encourages the separation of disciplines in an interdisciplinary world.
- It teachers kids to value extrinsic rather than intrinsic motivation
- It inspires grade inflation, which nullifies whatever value it might have had in the past to distinguish one student's performance from another.

(Mastery Transcript Consortium)

At the 2016 meeting Looney further added these limitations to the normal transcript and its impact on teaching and learning:

- Content knowledge valued over skills and character
- One to many teaching, not individualized
- Small time block schedules (assembly line)
- Academic silos
- "Seat Time" (Carnegie unit) based crediting
- More-is-better messaging to students (more APs, more extracurriculars, etc.)

(Looney, 2016)

Having established the "absurdities," of our system, Looney in his presentation then moved to the "atrocities" of the status quo—what are described on the website under the banner "School Shouldn't Hurt."

We hear it all the time, particularly from students themselves. School hurts. Too many students leave high school uninspired, under-prepared, and anxious about the world that awaits them.

Why? Our schools are tasked primarily with sorting and ranking them, rather than engaging and enlightening them. The current transcript reduces a complex human being to simple numbers and letters. We can do better.

(Mastery Transcript Consortium, n.d.)

Looney bolstered his argument with evidence from various studies indicating that students are sleeping too little, struggling with homework too much, experiencing depression and anxiety too often, and seeking mental health services in high school and college much more frequently. The studies showed that 89% of students reported high or extreme levels of academic pressure, while 85% reported feeling overwhelmed in college. Looney, bemoaning these trends and traumas while also acknowledging our collective culpability for this problem, cited Voltaire: "Those who can make you believe absurdities can make you commit atrocities" (Looney, 2016).

Looney's solution to all this was a new transcript and an organization to carry it forward, the Mastery Transcript Consortium; by 2018 it was an incorporated organization with multiple full-time professional employees. Looney proceeded to lay out the vision for how the new transcript would function, and how the organization would promote this transformation.

Looney presented the following vision for the MTC at the 2016 launch meeting, one that continues to drive its work.

Vision statement: The Mastery Transcript Consortium (MTC) is a collective of high schools organized around the development and dissemination of an alternative model of assessment, crediting and transcript generation. This model calls for students to demonstrate a mastery of skills, knowledge and habits of mind by presenting evidence that is then assessed against an institutionally specific standard of mastery.

This MTC model is substantively different from the traditional model of assessment that is typically organized around content oriented courses, Carnegie units for credit and A to F letter grades. The Mastery Transcript model is organized around performance areas (rather than academic departments), mastery standards and micro-credits (rather than letter grades). Each micro-credit applied to a transcript signifies complete mastery of a specific skill, knowledge block or habit of mind as defined by the crediting high school.

Simply put . . . the MTC hopes to change the relationship between preparation for college and college admissions for the betterment of students.

(Mastery Transcript Consortium, n.d.)

What do colleges say they need in a transcript? What are their must-haves? Looney had interviewed many college officials and sought to distill their needs into three simple bullet points, forming key constraints or design elements that the MTC must respect and meet:

- A transcript that is readable in under two minutes
- Differentiation of the strength of our students
- Clear understanding of the shape of the student (who are they?)

(Mastery Transcript Consortium, n.d.)

Looney also proposed Core Principles, which distinguish key aspects of the MTC.

1. No Required Standardization of Mastery Credits: The performance areas, credit standards (rubrics, etc.) and credits are specific only to the individual crediting school, and will never be standardized across schools.
2. No Grades: Letter grading (or numerical equivalent) will not be used.
3. Consistent Transcript Format: Transcript has to be readable by college admission officers (once trained) in less than two minutes. Therefore, the transcript format has to be reasonably consistent across MTC schools.

(Mastery Transcript Consortium, n.d.)

The insistence on no grades, and no stand-ins for grades, represents a radical divergence from the status quo and from many other competency-based learning programs. But, to Looney and the MTC leadership, something has to be done to relieve the pressure and stress, the competition and anxiety, the depression and self-harm that is happening in so many high schools in the US and elsewhere, and this is a way to combat that at its root.

What will the new, digitally powered, MTC transcript comprise? Looney visualized it for the audience using a three-layer structure. The top layer, the distilled student record first viewed by transcript reviewers, is deemed the "transcript/credits layer." A colorful display—some form of spider web chart or wheel, perhaps—would arrange students' achievements in each domain of mastery that the individual school has determined for its program. It is important for students to be able to distinguish themselves from others, and for colleges to effectively discriminate among applicants, and so it is critical that the new system be able to ensure students can demonstrate their unique qualities. Sometimes this is described as how students can display themselves as "spiky," rather than square. Accordingly, in each of the new transcript's four to ten domains, a student upon graduation will demonstrate that they have earned the threshold number of credits for all domains, but have considerably exceeded the minimum, gone above and beyond, in one or several of them to best show themselves for their distinguishing excellence, in a way perhaps better than in the current model (Looney, 2016).

At any time, a reader of the transcript's first layer could click on any domain (say, critical thinking and problem-solving, or quantitative reasoning) to access a second layer, which would reveal the standards and rubrics used by the school to hold students accountable and assess "mastery" in that domain. These, again, would be the individual school's responsibility to craft or select from a set of options, and would offer individual schools valuable opportunities to distinguish themselves, whether for the rigor of their standards, the creativity of their rubrics, or otherwise (Looney, 2016).

The third layer, the evidence/artifacts/"best work" level, might be the most important Here, students carefully curate their original work display their proficiency, or mastery, in that domain competency area. In stark contrast to the conventional contemporary high school transcript, readers won't need to rely upon the judgment of the teacher who awarded an A (or a C), but instead can, if they choose, see for themselves a student's work and confirm its quality. There's no obligation for any "mastery transcript" reader to click through beyond the top layer. Some will be far too busy; some will not feel the need to check; but some will find this an especially useful way to gain greater insight into candidates on the bubble between admission and rejection (Looney, 2016).

Looney offered examples of a more detailed flowchart of the process. Students create all kinds of work products and artifacts, which are ingested into a cloud-based data storage inventory. With an adviser, they sort and prioritize their work, receiving feedback about it regularly and revising accordingly. They then select and organize exemplary work, or perhaps a representative sampling of work, and transfer it into a new folder for review by a panel of teachers established to evaluate work according to standards and rubrics and awarded badges or credits/micro-credits for demonstrated mastery. Those submissions declined are returned with feedback derived from the rubrics. Approved credits and the accompanying evidence of mastery are then entered into the digital transcript, which is updated regularly as new credits are awarded, and can be, when needed, submitted via API to college or other readers (Looney, 2016).

The MTC's goal is to provide more authentic, interdisciplinary, apprenticeship-type learning and reduce student stress by moving beyond the limits of course credits and letter grades as markers of student accomplishment. During and since the initial 2016 MTC launch meeting, several other ideas and opportunities for shifting to a new transcript format have been proposed and embraced by educators. Among them:

- Social-emotional learning, (or noncognitive skills and character strengths) can be become competencies for credits on a mastery transcript, and as such, can then receive far greater attention in teaching and learning. Students can accumulate examples of persistence, resilience, or collaboration, tag and store them in their portfolios, and submit them for credits. This could be a powerful way to genuinely broaden educational outcomes and make more meaningful holistic, well-rounded, or "whole child" education at the secondary level. Colleges, too, would benefit, as they increasingly take note of the evidence-based value of these competencies for success in post-secondary education and careers. Students with earned and evidence-supported credits in these skills might rightfully receive bonus points in their application process.

- Out-of-school learning can far more easily be recognized and credited in this new system. In the conventional Carnegie unit transcript, it is hard to know what to do with a six-month internship in a congressional office, the year-long management of a substantial extracurricular enterprise (e.g. editing the school newspaper), or caregiving over many months for an elderly or infant relative. Now, credits can be fashioned for professionalism, leadership, or caregiving, and students can submit evidence of this out of school learning for recognition and credit.

- Reflection and integration of learning can become better supported. Kevin Mattingly, a longtime academic dean in secondary schools, has written that the MTC might provide, via the process of curating, receiving feedback, and submitting portfolios, an opportunity for students to be more reflective and integrative in their school studies and better see and track their growth over time in meaningful ways (Mattingly, 2017).

- Student agency may be enhanced. Mattingly has noted that, through the elimination of grades and the providing of credits for learning experiences outside traditional coursework, "students are more motivated and able to develop a sense of agency when they are able to pursue studies that have purpose and meaning for them that are not readily available in a traditional grades and transcript system." (Mattingly, 2017).

- Pace of learning can be better differentiated. Learning becomes more constant, and time more the variable. Students who can demonstrate and document mastery swiftly can get it done, and students needing more time to master a topic can take that time without compromising their academic record, as is usually the case at present. Chris Sturgis, writing at CompetencyWorks (comptencyworks.org) about the MTC, reinforces this point, saying that a fourth principle of the way the mastery transcript should work is: "Do not indicate how much time it takes someone to fulfill that credit" (Sturgis, 2018).

Looney's vision inspired me and many others at the initial MTC meetings, and the evidence of that inspiration is abundant. MTC membership has continued to grow swiftly, and membership entails significant annual dues. Shortly after its launch, MTC received a large foundation grant of two million dollars, with an obligation that that grant be matched over several years (Mastery Transcript Consortium, n.d.).

That said, there are aspects of what is described above that deserve some critical attention.

Is the two-minute rule too limiting? Looney explained that in conversations with college admission/enrollment officers, two minutes was the maximum that could be allotted by any post-secondary institution to the evaluation of a transcript. But to concede this point may be to concede too much. Already, the MTC intends to challenge higher ed admissions with its new format—and for the new transcript format to have the meaningful transformative impact it aspires to, perhaps it has to demand also more time and attention. To appreciate the student portfolio samples, to understand the rigors of the rubrics, to evaluate how students have met all minimum thresholds and also gone deep into particular competency areas: this might take more than two minutes, and maybe that also should asked of higher ed.

Is the featured freedom to schools to define their own credits creating too great a diversity of form? The MTC's first core principle is admirable, democratic, inclusive. Clearly there is every intent to not dictate mandates about what must be taught and learned. But without any commonality of credits, won't higher ed admission officers be that much more uncertain about how to treat these transcripts, and how to have confidence in student preparation? Shouldn't there be a "common core" of what is most important for student learning in these critical years? Surely there could be a compromise approach to this first principle, with some standardization established about what performance areas and credits are required. And—to go one step forward—surely there should be some minimum thresholds for competencies in each critical domain, such as numeracy and literacy. Recall that among the sharpest criticisms of the New Zealand NCEA was that its required elements were too few (as explained in the *Spoiled by Choice* report), and at least NCEA had some mandated minimums.

And finally, when one looks at the MTC vision statement and three principles, one can't help but wonder whether there is not enough attention to teaching and learning. Nearly every aspect of these four statements addresses crediting and transcript elements exclusively, with the partial exception of the end of the vision statement. Now, it is clear from other statements that Looney intends that the new transcript and crediting be the tail that wags the dog—that a different defined set and documentation of outcomes of a high school education will influence in a "backwards design" manner curriculum and instruction. But this important element is left only implicit, too much so, in these high-level, defining statements: there should be greater attention to the shift in teaching and learning, described with some specifics, that the new system is intended to create.

The organizational structure of the MTC corporation is for the most part beyond the scope of this discussion, but certain aspects should be briefly summarized. Looney explained the importance of creating and managing a strong organization to support the development and implementation of such a dramatic change to high school crediting and documentation. It is intended to provide the following roles:

1. Development of an alternative assessment, crediting and transcript model
2. Professional development for teachers and administrators
3. Organizational and program assistance
4. Development of a technology platform
5. Advocacy/communications with Colleges and Universities
6. Public Relations/Communications

(Looney, 2016)

One of the most hotly disputed elements of the MTC as an organization has been its initial decision to form an exclusive membership for independent private schools only, excluding public and other types of high schools. As Looney clarified:

> The MTC hopes to use the collective influence, access and flexibility of established independent schools to change the college preparation model for all high schools . . . not just private schools. However, we are starting with just independent schools to minimize complication and maximize our initial influence in partnership with college presidents and admission deans.
>
> (Looney, 2016)

This author, and many other educators, vigorously challenged this initial policy. However, it should be noted that as of this writing in 2019, MTC membership has been opened to all types of secondary schools, and its membership is rapidly being expanded to include public education organizations.

In the wake of its debut in 2016, the MTC received news coverage from outlets such as the *Washington Post*, *Christian Science Monitor*, *Inside Higher Ed*, the *Washington Post*, and many others. There are few common threads in this coverage. Some are enthusiastic about the potential, such as a *Forbes* column which states that the MTC initiative:

does suggest a very real desire to provide a fuller picture of each student, one that a simple number or letter can't. It would also in theory enable college admission officers to see each applicant more clearly, enabling better decision making.

(Dix, 2017)

Other articles are less enthusiastic; some focus on the private school exclusivity of the consortium, some on skepticism that colleges will be able to adapt themselves to such a major change, and others on whether students and parents will themselves be willing to adapt.

Two pieces of coverage explore key issues with which every educator should grapple when exploring retooled grading and crediting: equity and quality. In the *Washington Post*, columnist Catherine Rampell posits that the MTC and its general model could further advantage the already advantaged students who attend prominent and affluent schools. Her analysis operates on two levels: one easy to see, the other somewhat more sophisticated and subtle. Students, Rampell notes, will require additional attention, advising, and support from teachers, counselors, and educator-evaluators to effectively manage their MTC journey. This includes high-quality, apprentice-like learning opportunities that would generate the impressive artifacts that students would enter into their MTC portfolios. This also includes assistance in the work of curation: sorting, prioritizing, revising. How likely is it that students in severely underserved and underfunded communities would have access to this kind of assistance? (Rampell, 2017).

Rampell also addresses critically the MTC's second core principle: no grades of any kind. Elite post-secondary institutions, she explains, have in recent decades sharply diminished the "signaling" that their course grades can provide, particularly by grade inflation, but also by other devices such as narratives and alternate formats (Rampell, 2017).

It's no surprise that elite schools have been less diligent at combating grade inflation. In fact, game theory predicts it. If you're a top-ranked school, having more "noise" in your grading system reduces the ability of potential employers (or admissions officers) to accurately judge particular students. On average, this can boost your school's job/admissions placement rate. That's because the impressive school name does the work of signaling a student's abilities, rather than a more finely grained assessment of the student's actual abilities.

By contrast, lower-ranked schools really want superstars to stand out, lest they get written off because of the less-elite brand. To be sure, students at these lesser-ranked institutions are still pressuring grades upward, but administrators know they need some segmentation at the very top.

(Rampell, 2017)

It can't be disputed that the MTC has been launched and is being led, at least until recently, exclusively by some of the most elite schools in the US. As access to the most selective universities becomes ever narrower, Rampell sees elite schools using "game theory" to restructure their reporting such that their students can be viewed primarily as products of their "impressive schooling" (be it real or perceived) and not evaluated as easily or with more scrutiny by their individual qualifications. Rampell does not speculate whether these schools might be using "game theory" consciously and deliberately to maximize the competitive advantage of their students in admission, and I have been close enough to many inside conversations to state with confidence that they are not. But her point is worthy of consideration regardless: the impacts, not the intentions, of transformative movements matter most.

There are multiple responses to the Rampell critique. The MTC will soon be open to a far wider array of schools, and in 2018 engaged a public school superintendent to direct outreach and promote more inclusivity. Schools with high free and reduced lunch populations may receive discounts on consortium membership dues. It will be important, as this proceeds, for the MTC as an organization to generate and provide resources to support all of its members, regardless of financial status, to make this transition. To Rampell's second point, one could argue that the signaling of letter grades in elite/affluent schools is already near zero; many or most students in these schools already present themselves to the Ivy League with 4.1 GPAs and half a dozen AP courses. How different is no-grades from near-identical grades in the signaling she describes? The MTC, via its intended "third layer" of curated student work, will provide college readers—at least those with the time to study the third layer—more, not fewer, opportunities to conduct what Rampell calls (and called for) a "more finely grained assessment of the student's actual abilities." Consider the difference between a conventional transcript presenting nearly or entirely identical course sequence and grades, and a "mastery transcript" that presents more differentiated quantities of credits in key learning domains, complete with instant access to sample student work. There's no question that the latter offers the reader far more insight to distinguish applicants.

Regarding quality: Tom Vander Ark, on his Getting Smart website, presented a particularly perceptive response to the MTC in September 2017. Calling it a "fantastic development," he writes that it is "part of a megatrend toward a show what you know economy where demonstrated capabilities are more important than traditional pedigrees" (Vander Ark, 2017).

Looking closely at competency-based credentialing, though, he raises two issues about quality. One: if and when the MTC expands widely, "quality control may become an issue at scale . . . when 10,000 schools are on the platform, some weak forms of evidence will be posted and it could lead to the next version of evidence inflation." Two: "as automated feedback systems get better at polishing every form of student work there will be machine-reduced variability in student work product, thereby reducing the value of relying on underlying work product as the guarantee of competence" (Vander Ark, 2017).

The MTC doesn't put a lot of emphasis on its online communications and public presentations, at least as of the time of this writing, on quality. Most of its messaging attends to the failings of the status quo transcript, the stress on students, the value and appeal of an apprenticeship model of learning, the opportunity to do more to assess and credit key skills (including noncognitive factors), and the way schools can design and implement competency-based systems and transcripts. But as we've seen in the previous chapter, looking at Western Governors University and the New Zealand NCEA program, educators advocating and implementing this major shift owe it to their students and the success of their own initiatives to be rigorous and vigilant about the quality of student work and the depth of student learning.

The Mastery Transcript Consortium will not be, this book predicts, a flash in the pan, a short-lived and swiftly forgotten experiment. Its leadership is vigorous, well informed, passionate, and well connected; its membership is swiftly growing; its finances seem sound. The bet being placed here is that in twenty years, the MTC transcript will be as well known and widely influential on US secondary school education as, say, the Advanced Placement system is. And if the MTC per se doesn't thrive, the model of competency-based crediting it exemplifies will still likely become a much larger presence in the US secondary school landscape.

The MTC can be understood as two different things: the consortium, specific nonprofit corporation and organization with an executive director and board of directors; and the MTC transcript, the specific trademarked and patented digital transcript and portfolio system that collects data from students, aggregates and organizes it at the school level, and presents it to colleges. The remainder of this book is intended to assist educators aspiring to understand and prepare themselves and their schools for participation in the MTC or in other competency-based crediting and transcript transformations.

References

Dintersmith, T. (2018). *What School Could Be: Insights and Inspiration from Teachers Across America*. Princeton, NJ: Princeton University Press.

Dix, W. (2017, May 22). A Proposal to Radically Revise High School Transcripts May Alter College Admission. Retrieved September 16, 2018, from www.forbes.com/sites/willarddix/2017/05/22/a-proposal-to-radically-revise-high-school-transcripts-may-alter-college-admission/#100e49321da3

Looney, S. (2016, April 28). Mastery Transcript Consortium. Presentation presented at Mastery Transcript Consortium Meeting in Cleveland Botanical Garden, Cleveland, Ohio.

Mastery Transcript Consortium. (n.d.). Retrieved September 16, 2018, from www.mastery.org/

Mattingly, K. (2017, August 1). Reasons for Joining the MTC and Some Ways to Go Forward (Memo). New York, NY.

Rampell, C. (2017, May 11). Opinion | Why Getting Rid of Grades Would Help Rich Students – and Hurt Poor Ones. Retrieved September 16, 2018, from www.washingtonpost.com/opinions/why-getting-rid-of-grades-would-help-rich-students--and-hurt-poor-ones/2017/05/11/b038f90c-3683-11e7-b4ee-434b6d506b37_story.html

Sturgis, C. (2018, May 20). Mastery Credits? Mastery Transcript? (Web log post). Retrieved September 16, 2018, from www.competencyworks.org/k-12-higher-education/mastery-credits-mastery-transcript/

Vander Ark, T. (2017, September 17). School Consortium Proposes a Better Transcript. Retrieved September 16, 2018, from www.gettingsmart.com/2017/09/school-consortium-proposes-a-better-transcript/

4

Elements of the New Model

New transcript models, organized around credits for competencies or providing "mastery credits," rather than Carnegie units for traditional course completion, will require careful attention to five topics:

A. Defining and illustrating competencies and how they are developed.
B. Establishing learning opportunities by which students can earn competencies.
C. Collecting and curating student work in digital portfolios.
D. Assessing competencies, particularly with rubrics.
E. Using new transcript types to report earned competencies.

A. Defining Competencies

Competency-based crediting systems demand clarity about the definition of a competency. The work of transforming our schools can easily go awry when the definitions become too slippery and the language too confusing.

Rose Colby in her book *Competency-Based Education* writes that a competency is a "student's ability to apply clusters of standards to execute a particular performance task." Competencies should be "demanding, aligned to standards, concept-based, and assessable" (Colby, 2017).

Critical to this work is distinguishing competencies from standards. In a thorough discussion published by the website RedesignU, competencies and standards are distinguished across multiple dimensions, including these five: context and purpose; grain size; focus; gradation; and implications for assessment (Schaef, 2016).

Context and Purpose

Standards emerged to become more prominent in the 1990s as a vehicle by which educational systems and curricula could be standardized, tested, measured, and compared. Although many educators use them to positive effect, and, when used well, they can be hugely valuable for instructional design and assessment, standards also have been used in ways that have narrowed student learning and led to overtesting.

Standards are derived by slicing learning content into thin wedges or widgets; competencies, however, are drawn from looking out into the world and identifying what combinations of knowledge and skills are needed to perform a task.

> Competencies are being developed from a much more aspirational and contextualized place than that of academic standards. School communities, districts, and states are creating competencies that encompass the knowledge, skills, and dispositions needed for purposeful, meaningful, and productive life in the world beyond school.
>
> (Schaef, 2016)

Grain Size

> Standards are smaller than competencies; standards are intended to be more like atoms, discrete units, whereas competencies are more molecular, representing logical and coherent combinations of standards (atoms) and also additional components of application and transfer.
>
> (Schaef, 2016)

Focus

"Standards tend to focus more on content knowledge (though there are exceptions), whereas competencies focus more on skills, application, and impact" (Schaef, 2016).

Gradations

> The order in which standards are learned often bears little importance; competencies are more often organized into progressions from lesser to greater complexity and challenge. Competencies are

not "one and done," like many standards, which are course-based and attached to specific grade levels or bands.

(Schaef, 2016)

Implications for Assessment

Standards are often assessed via questions (often multiple choice) that demand only remembering and comprehension. Multiple choice will not serve for competencies which usually demand higher orders of thinking on Bloom's taxonomy or Webb's Depth of Knowledge; accordingly assessing competencies usually demands performances not just bubble tests.

(Schaef, 2016)

Where Will the Competencies for Which Students Are Credited Come From?

Competency credit "banks" may be established at the network, district, or other level. In some cases, it may be that schools and the teachers therein have no responsibility or opportunity to define or create competencies. As in New Zealand, the set of competencies available may be defined by a higher authority (district, state, network, etc.). We can expect that in the US, as in New Zealand, competency credit "banks" will become increasingly available, and the work of establishing a school's set of competencies will be largely one of curation, not creation This will aid in efficiency for educators, higher quality for establishing the most important elements of student learning, and greater ease of recognition and utilization by higher education admission officers and employers.

In many cases, though, educators in the coming years will have the challenging but interesting work to define competencies at their school level. When going about this work, educators can draw from many wells, including conventional academic domains, defined skill sets such as twenty-first-century or social-emotional, and other areas. ACT, best known for its college admission test, has conducted extensive research into the constituent elements of success in schooling, college, careers, and life generally. The ACT Holistic Framework is organized into four domains that could be of great use when considering the various "wells" from which to draw competencies: core academic skills, including Math, Science, Reading, and Writing; cross-cutting competencies, including critical thinking; social-emotional skills, including sustaining effort, getting along with others, and maintaining composure; and career-navigation skills. This comprehensive framework is broken into detailed components, subcomponents, skills, and performance level descriptors (Camara et al., 2015).

Many educators will typically begin with what they are most familiar with—conventional courses they have taught—and break them into key competencies. Competency grain sizes will vary, but schools that expect students to achieve eight to twelve competency credits in a year can on that basis anticipate that a conventional year-long course might yield two to three competencies. In New Zealand, however, students earn eighty credits a year, and accordingly the conversion for a typical school-year course would yield more like ten to fifteen.

Teachers should identify a course's or a unit's big idea or enduring understanding, or should review the standards associated with that course and combine them into larger conceptual clusters especially valuable for lasting understanding. They should then determine how this big idea can be applied and transferred in a vigorous and rigorous way to a challenging task that has some degree, the higher the better, of authenticity in order to craft the competency statement.

High-quality, overarching competencies will also come from the school's faculty and leadership jointly, not just from the individual courses. Indeed, it might be wiser to start here: look to the school's history, values, mission, and philosophy, and determine collectively what are the hallmarks of a graduate of this particular school (or district). Survey alumni and parents, ask board members to weigh in, and explore with students. Then, generate a finite set of core competencies associated with the individual school. Among other things, this process ought to allow schools far greater opportunities to meaningfully differentiate themselves from others and provide genuine choice to families and students. (See the way this process played out at Putney School in Chapter 6.)

The state of New Hampshire, the nation's competency-based education leader, has designed and published a competency "validation rubric" that can be used both to inform the design of a competency and then to evaluate the effectiveness of that design. It evaluates competencies on four criteria:

- Relevance to content area: To what extent does this competency statement align with standards, leading students to conceptual understanding of content?
- Enduring Concepts: To what extent does this competency statement reflect enduring concepts?

- Cognitive Demand: What depth of knowledge does this competency statement promote?
- Relative to Assessment: To what extent does the competency statement promote opportunities for students to demonstrate evidence of learning?

(NHDOE for NH State Board of Education, 2010)

Note that this rubric is not of universal value; it operates, as does the NH model generally, in a mode that ties competencies far more closely to coursework and academic standards than does the approach or model in this book. The first criterion, specifically, does not always apply to all types of competencies and competency credits. It does offer good value, though, for those subsets of competencies and credits drawn particularly from academic subjects.

One concern or criticism of competency-based education is that it may result in the lowering of intellectual standards, the softening of rigor, and the reduction of cognitive demand. Educators should strive to write rubrics in ways that offset this concern and demonstrate demanding cognitive applications. Bloom's taxonomy, Webb's Depth of Knowledge, or Hess's Cognitive Rigor Matrix are useful tools to employ in design to ensure that students are thinking and performing at high levels when being assessed. The NH rubric explains that higher levels of cognitive demand entail a competency that:

- Asks students to create conceptual connections and exhibit a level of understanding that is beyond the stated facts or literal interpretation and defend their position or point of view through application of content.
- Promotes complex connections through creating, analyzing, designing, proving, developing, or formulating.

(NHDOE for NH State Board of Education, 2010)

Most readers are already familiar with Bloom's Taxonomy; it bears fruit to return to that resource regularly. Even experienced educators can find it valuable to ask themselves again, when preparing or revising a task or test, whether students are being asked to do more than "apply" their learning. What more would this assignment entail for students to analyze deeply, evaluate critically, create originally? Bring this into competency design and evaluation, as well.

Webb's Depth of Knowledge (DOK) and Hess's Cognitive Rigor Matrix might be less familiar, but are also pertinent to this work of designing and auditing competencies for rigorous thinking. Competencies should be written at the third Webb DOK level ("reasoning and planning, complex and abstract thinking, defending and reasoning required") or the fourth ("make real world applications in new settings, has multiple answers or approaches, often requires extended period of time with multiple steps") (Amidon, Monroe, & Ortwein, n.d.).

The Cognitive Rigor Matrix (CRM) brings Bloom's and Webb's together in two axes for a framework that allows instructional designers and assessors to consider and determine more specifically the rigor of their tasks. Using the CRM, educators designing or evaluating the rigor of competencies would look closely at the bottom-right four boxes, and apply to their competency design a rubric such as "verify reasonableness of results; justify or critique conclusions drawn; apply understanding in a novel way; develop a complex model for a given situation; develop an alternate solution; articulate a new theme, knowledge, or perspective" (Hess, 2018).

The Mastery Transcript Consortium in its very name emphasizes that credits will be awarded not simply for "competency," but for mastery. A popular, and powerful, definition of mastery comes from the late, great Grant Wiggins:

> Mastery is effective transfer of learning in authentic and worthy performance. Students have mastered a subject when they are fluent, even creative, in using their knowledge, skills, and understanding in key performance challenges and contexts at the heart of that subject, as measured against valid and high standards.
>
> (Wiggins, 1989)

This standard for mastery is a high one, but very much worthy of aspiration to in the work of designing competencies.

Sample Model Competency Credits

In this example of competency credits, students are required to complete all Foundational Credit requirements for graduation. Students are also expected to earn some, but not all, of the available Advanced Credits offered by the school.

Foundational Credits include evidence of learning, including some level of transfer, and must be earned prior to graduation.

Advanced Credits require extended engagement and more significant evidence of transfer.

1. Creativity

Sample Foundational Credits

a. Synthesis: Student can connect ideas in new or different ways and generate new approaches to problems by combining and adapting existing approaches.

b. Incorporating Diverse Perspectives: Student can be open and responsive to new and diverse perspectives; incorporate group input and feedback into the work (Partnership for 21st Century Skills, 2009).

Sample Advanced Credits

c. Problem-finding and Prototyping: Student can identify, frame, and thoroughly evaluate the underlying causes and presenting issues of a problem found in their local community (or an environment they visit and engage with), and can then undertake a multi-step, extended process of analysis and problem-solving, culminating in a prototype that effectively addresses the identified problem and presents to an expert or involved audience.

d. Innovation: Student can act on creative ideas to make a tangible and useful contribution to the field in which the innovation will occur (Partnership for 21st Century Skills, 2009).

e. Artistic Creation: Student can originate or substantially develop in an extended way an artistic performance that is innovative and accomplishes its purpose for an intended audience (McTighe, 2013).

2. Critical Thinking

Sample Foundational Mastery Credits

a. Evaluating Claims: Student can analyze and evaluate evidence, arguments, claims and beliefs, and major alternative points of view (Partnership for 21st Century Skills, 2009).

b. Information Literacy: Student can locate, organize, analyze, critically evaluate (refute, prove), synthesize, and ethically use information from a variety of sources and media (ISTE, 2007).

c. Problem-Solving: Student can evaluate authentic problems, identify and devise multiple solutions, and evaluate and compare solutions using trial and error, prototyping, and other methods.

Sample Advanced Mastery Credits

d. Advanced Research: Student can identify and define authentic problems and significant questions for inquiry and investigation (ISTE, 2007).

e. Advanced Data Interpretation: Student can collect and analyze data to identify potential strategies and solutions; develop, expand upon, and test interpretations; and effectively evaluate advantages and disadvantages of interpretations, strategies, and prototypes (ISTE, 2007).

3. Communication

Sample Foundational Mastery Credits

a. Listening Skills: Student can listen attentively, with discernment and openness, mindful of filters/biases, and incorporate feedback and ideas from others (Hewlett Foundation, 2013; NAIS, 2010).

b. Language Proficiency: Student can understand and express ideas in two or more languages (NAIS, 2010).

c. Oral Fluency: Student can speak persuasively and engagingly, with understanding of and respect for diverse audiences.

d. Writing Proficiency: Student can write clearly and concisely to communicate complex concepts for a variety of audiences (Hewlett Foundation, 2013).

Sample Advanced Mastery Credits

e. Virtuoso Communication: Student can develop and present with a combination of oral, written, and video techniques an original message in a novel way that is published or presented on a public platform and effectively moves an audience to a different understanding or emotional state in a substantial and lasting way.

4. Collaboration

Sample Foundational Mastery Credits

    a.   Collaboration in Groups: Student can work as part of a group to identify group goals, and collaborate with others to complete tasks and solve problems successfully (Hewlett Foundation, 2013).

    b.   Cultural Competency: Student can learn from, and work collaboratively with, individuals from diverse cultures, religions, and lifestyles in a spirit of mutual respect and open dialogue (Partnership for 21st Century Skills, 2009).

Sample Advanced Mastery Credits

    c.   Leveraging Diversity: Student can effectively engage with those of diverse backgrounds when confronting complex challenges, and in an extended way, leverage different, varying, and competing social and cultural perspectives and approaches to create new ideas and advance upon those challenges (Partnership for 21st. Century Skills, 2009).

    d.   Extended Leadership: Student can lead a team, individually or collaboratively, over an extended time toward achieving a challenging goal by articulating purpose, motivating and engaging the strengths of all team-members, resolving conflicts, and managing timelines.

5. Self-Directed Learning

Sample Foundational Mastery Credits

    a.   Goal-Setting and Adaptation: Student can consistently set goals for learning tasks, monitor their progress towards the goal, and adapt their approach as needed to successfully complete a task or solve a novel, complex, and/or real world problem (Hewlett Foundation, 2013).

    b.   Persistence: Student can persist through difficulties, delay gratification, refocus after distractions, and maintain momentum until they reach their goal, use failures and setbacks as opportunities for feedback, and apply lessons learned to improve future efforts (Hewlett Foundation, 2013).

    c.   Mastery Mindset: Student cares about the quality of work and puts in extra effort to do things thoroughly, uses growth and mastery mindset strategies effectively, and continues looking for new ways to learn challenging material or solve difficult problems (Hewlett Foundation, 2013).

Sample Advanced Mastery Credits

d. Agility in Ambiguity: Student can demonstrate flexibility, agility, and adaptability when undertaking complex tasks, can work effectively in a climate of ambiguity and changing priorities, can view failure as an opportunity to learn, and acknowledges that innovation involves small successes and frequent mistakes (NAIS, 2010).

e. Curation and Reflection: Student can thoughtfully curate a portfolio of learning and is able to effectively reflect on one's own evidence of learning—to self-assess work in order to determine what is learned and what needs to be learned (NAIS, 2010).

6. Humanities and Arts

History and Social Sciences

Sample Foundational Mastery Credits

a. Historical Research Basics: Student can gather information from primary and secondary sources to evaluate historical claims and make historical interpretations (McTighe, 2013).

b. Using History: Student can apply knowledge of major eras, enduring themes, turning points, and historic influences to analyze the forces of continuity and change in the community, region, nation-state, and world (Henry County (GA) Schools, n.d.).

c. Global Analysis: Student can analyze the physical, human, and environmental geography of various regions of the world to evaluate the interdependent relationships and challenges facing human systems in the past, present, and future (Henry County (GA) Schools, n.d.).

Sample Advanced Mastery Credits

d. Local Issue Policy-influencing: Student can question, research, present, and defend discipline-based processes and knowledge from civics, government, economics, geography, and history in authentic contexts in order to apply the attributes of a responsible and active citizen to affect a real-world issue based on a local need (Henry County (GA) Schools, n.d.).

e. Prediction Using Historical Insight: Student can make predictions for current or future events or issues based on extensive research and understanding of related historical patterns and can use appropriate evidence to defend predictions (McTighe, 2013).

Arts
Sample Foundational Mastery Credits

a. Evaluating Art: Student can apply the skills and language of a specific arts discipline to evaluate how artworks convey meaning by perceiving and analyzing artistic work; interpret intent and meaning of artistic work; and apply criteria to artistic work (New Hampshire Department of Education, 2012).

b. Conveying Artistic Meaning: Student can apply the skills and language of a specific arts discipline to convey meaning and communicate ideas of completed works by analyzing, interpreting, and selecting artistic works for presentation, and by realizing, developing, and refining artistic works for presentation (New Hampshire Department of Education, 2012).

Sample Advanced Mastery Credits

c. Making Artistic Meaning: Student can apply the skills and language of a specific arts discipline to relate personal meaning and external context to specific works of art and during the art-making process by synthesizing and relating knowledge and experience to artistic ideas and artistic work and applying societal, cultural, and historical contexts to artistic ideas and artistic work.

English and Language Arts
Sample Foundational Mastery Credits

a. Reading Literature Competency: Student can demonstrate the ability to comprehend, analyze, and critique a variety of increasingly complex print and non-print literary texts (New Hampshire Department of Education, 2012).

b. Reading Informational Texts Competency: Student can demonstrate the ability to comprehend, analyze, and critique a variety of increasingly complex print and non-print informational texts—including science, social studies, and technical subjects (New Hampshire Department of Education, 2012).

c. Writing Arguments and Explanatory Writing Competency: Student can demonstrate the ability to analyze and critique texts or topics and support claims and reasoning with sufficient evidence for intended purpose and audience, and demonstrates the ability to effectively write informative texts to examine and convey complex ideas for a variety of purposes and audiences (New Hampshire Department of Education, 2012).

Sample Advanced Mastery Credits

d. Literary Research and Interpretation: Student can research and write a cogent, persuasive, and publishable opinion piece on a matter of general public or academic importance and value (Bassett, 2009).

e. Creating Literature: Student can apply knowledge of language structure, figurative language, and genre to create extended and complex print and non-print texts (NCTE, 2012).

7. Science, Technology, Engineering, and Mathematics

Sample Foundational Mastery Credits

a. Algebraic Reasoning: Student can make use of patterns, relations, and functions to interpret, compare, and analyze pure and applied situations, using the information to make conjectures and support conclusions (New Hampshire Department of Education, 2012).

b. Mathematical Modeling: Student can conceptualise, generalise and utilise information based on their investigations and modeling of problems, and can link different information sources and representations and flexibly translate between them (OECD, 2013).

c. Geometric Reasoning: Student can solve problems involving spatial reasoning using properties of 2- and 3-dimensional figures to analyze, represent, and model geometric relationships in pure/theoretical and authentic, applied contexts (New Hampshire Department of Education, 2012).

d. Evaluate claims: Student can evaluate a scientific claim, and critique experimental design or conclusions.

e. Observe Patterns: Student can observe patterns of forms and events, guide organization and classification, and prompt questions about relationships and the factors that influence them (NGSS, n.d.).

f. Investigate Causes: Student can investigate and explain causal relationships and the mechanisms by which they are mediated, test them across given contexts, and use them to predict and explain events in new contexts (NGSS, n.d.).

g. Structural Analysis: Student can define the way in which an object or living thing is shaped and how its substructure determines its properties and functions, and can apply that definition to predict and explain the shapes and structures of previously unstudied objects and living things (NGSS, n.d.).

Sample Advanced Mastery Credits

h. Mathematical Reasoning: Student can apply mathematical insight and understanding with a mastery of symbolic and formal mathematical operations and relationships to develop new approaches and strategies for attacking novel, complex, "poorly structured" problems and situations (OECD, 2013).

i. Statistical Reasoning: Student can apply statistical methods and reasoning to summarize, represent, analyze, and interpret categorical and quantitative data, including addressing authentic, applied scenarios, and can apply the rules of probability to determine the likelihood of a given outcome or to make decisions (New Hampshire Department of Education, 2012).

j. Scientific Investigation: Student can demonstrate the ability to work collaboratively and individually to define problems and generate testable questions, plan and conduct investigations using a variety of research methods in a various settings, analyze and interpret data, reason with evidence to construct explanations in light of existing theory and previous research and effectively communicate the research processes and conclusions (New Hampshire Department of Education, 2012).

k. Scientific Analysis: Student can analyze current issues involving science and technology to reach a decision or pose a solution to a problem, using scientific reasoning and evidence (McTighe, 2013).

B. Earning Competencies

All are familiar with how most students today earn high school credits. They attend all or most days of a school year, sit in a classroom for thirty to seventy-five minutes, take notes as a teacher talks and displays slides or writes on a black or whiteboard, complete small homework assignments, take periodic tests, and complete a final exam. In English classes, there are occasional essays; in science, occasional lab reports. Sometimes there are "term paper" assignments of some extended challenge, time, duration, and length, but not often. Teachers assign grades, sometimes 0–100, sometimes A–F or 0–4, average them in some simple formula, and students are assigned the letter grade their averaged graded work has "earned" them.

How will this differ in the alternative being proposed? We can look at this with a table showing where the learning will take place and how the credits will be earned.

Where learning occurs	How credits might be earned		
	By successful completion of a single culminating task of some substance	By passing of external exam, credential, certification, or badge	By the accumulation of and effective reflection upon a set of itemized and tagged pieces of evidence
In a classroom	Well suited: Extended term paper demanding original research and multiple iterations; Documentary-style video; Thesis-defense; formal presentation	Moderately well suited: a national-level critical thinking exam such as the College Work Readiness Assessment; perhaps some AP or IB exams; tech-company certifications	Moderately well suited: as explained below
In an online class	Not well suited	Moderately suited, depending on availability	Moderately suited
In an extracurricular program	Partially suited: i.e. publication of an edited student paper, direction of a play	Sometimes suited: Eagle Scout badge as example	
In work, service, or family caregiving	Not well suited	Not well suited	Well suited: as explained below

Where

As in the conventional school approach, competency credits can be earned by students taking a typical course, such as US History, though it would be retooled to award credits for historical competency, not class completion.

Students can also earn their credits through extracurricular experiences. Participation in activities such as student government, model UN, robotics, theater, journalism, and literary journals are often deep and lasting learning experiences, and it seems shortsighted of schools not to appreciate the significance of this learning and credit students with the competencies earned before sending them on to colleges or the workforce.

Beyond the school site, there are other environments in which students grow, develop skills, gain new understandings, and establish new competencies. Often, these are in jobs or internships, but they can also be found in extended service activities that go beyond simple tasks (such as typical community service actions like cleaning up a park or serving food in a soup kitchen). This can occur within a student's household itself; some students, particularly from disadvantaged circumstances, often spend many hours a week caretaking for younger siblings or elderly family members, and in doing so develop caregiving, management, and persistence competency.

How

Recall that competencies are defined as demanding higher-order thinking, transfer of knowledge and skills to novel scenarios, and performance. Multiple-choice, short-answer, and even most medium-length essays and lab reports are simply insufficient to demonstrate this kind of competency or mastery.

In his book, *Demonstrating Student Mastery with Digital Badges and Portfolios*, digital portfolio expert David Niguidula dedicates a full chapter to the importance of examining the high quality, demanding tasks that ought to be required of students as they build portfolios and earn badges. "Badges gain their credibility from the evidence behind them . . . Students, teachers, and other reviewers all need to be convinced by the submitted evidence" (Niguidula, 2019).

A: The first and perhaps most self-evident method by which students ate competency is by extended projects of some depth, often :formance tasks, such as

/

- research-driven term paper involving original research, primary document review and multiple versions;
- an inquiry-driven science experiment that includes designing the experiment, researching related studies, running the experiment multiple times or over an extended period;
- staging a theatrical production; directing a short documentary film; creating a comprehensive website; and so much more.

This performance task methodology works well with classroom learning, when teachers design and assess such tasks. Extracurricular experiences sometimes lend themselves very well to performance tasks, as itemized above, in the form of producing a play or publishing a literary journal, for example. Performance tasks are somewhat harder to produce in most jobs, service learning experiences, or home-family learning experiences, and so are moderately less well suited.

B: One alternative is the possibility of an externally administered and assessed exam, assessment, certification, credentialing, or badging. If these external assessments are of sufficient rigor and can be effectively aligned to an existing competency, they might effectively serve this purpose. Readers will recall that the New Zealand system awards a large proportion of credits via its national examinations.

Consider a school with a critical thinking/analytic reasoning competency credit. The Council for Aid to Education administers nationally the College Work Readiness Assessment (CWRA), which entails a roughly 75-minute essay task, interpreting multiple sources of evidence and applying them to a complex, real-work simulated task. It is assessed with a comprehensive and detailed rubric and held to a high standard. The exam awards badges for high-level performance, and it is perfectly reasonable to think that the earning of such a badge could qualify for the awarding of an aligned competency credit.

An Eagle Scout badge could also qualify for a leadership or similar type of credit. Earning a technical proficiency certificate from Microsoft or other such technology-company-associated credentials might fit well to a school-defined competency credit, as well.

What about an AP or IB exam? This will likely be a point of contention in some schools and school systems. In many cases, these exams seem too tied to a course rather than to a specific competency; often they don't ask of students genuine performances that entail transfer or application. But it is possible that some among this set of exams, such as AP Capstone, Studio Arts, or Calculus, might qualify; this will have to be determined individually by schools.

C: A third approach uses the accumulation of multiple items or artifacts of evidence over time. In the course of a school year, a student might assemble dozens of short and medium-length samples of work—short assignments, classroom presentations, tested tasks—that all represent demonstrated and growing proficiency in a particular competency. Feedback a student receives from teachers or others—club advisers, coaches, employers—specific to that competency might also be collected. At year's end or some other moment in time, a student might collect and review the accumulated evidence and, in freeform or by using a template, distill the many pieces into a single reflection and case statement for the earned credit. The accumulated evidence and the case statement and reflection would then be reviewed by a teacher or small panel that would award, if persuaded, the credit. Readers will recall a system like this in place at the Lerner Medical College in Cleveland.

This last methodology has many advantages. It allows students more easily to aggregate learning and work products from across multiple learning spaces—classroom, online, extracurriculars, and work/service/home—toward earning a particular credit. It is also more suited than the others to recognizing learning in spaces outside the conventional teacher-led classroom spaces.

In all three methods teaching and learning needs to be designed and orchestrated such that skills are developed and opportunities are provided for students to tackle complex tasks, demonstrate deep understanding, perform high-level skills, display strong personal attributes, and generate meaningful evidence of the preceding.

Progressive, constructivist, or experiential pedagogical strategies can inform and support this shift. In *Understanding by Design* (UbD), Wiggins and McTighe guide educators in clearly and emphatically establishing the intended outcomes of any learning unit, which educators can use to ensure that competencies for which students are expected to gain credit are front and center. Phase two of UbD entails clarifying what work products students will generate that demonstrate they have indeed acquired those competencies. These defined work products can be used either as culminating singular performances for our first method, or they can be a collection of smaller tasks that together are accumulated for a portfolio of learning evidence. It is only after the learning outcomes and the demonstrations of learning are determined that the plan of learning is made in the UbD model (Wiggins & McTighe, 2008).

Project-based learning (PBL) is a second variant on this theme. PBL, as defined by the leading PBL organization the Buck Institute of Education, similarly works backwards from specific defined outcomes to plan aligned products or performances, and then implements a careful series of steps including introducing, defining, and acquiring needed knowledge and skills, extended inquiry, drafts and revisions, and reflection.

McTighe recommends for performance task design a model he calls GRASPS. Define for students a "Real-World **G**oal" (design a new community center for your town); assign them a "Real-World **R**ole" (architect or mayor or community center director); identify a "Real-World **A**udience" (the town council, a neighborhood association, the current community center staff); pose a "Real-World **S**ituation" (bored teenagers, elderly loneliness); ask for "Real-World **P**roducts or Performances" (renderings of models of new community center, presentation or video explaining its value); and ensure alignments to **S**tandards (McTighe, 2013).

Design thinking (DT) is fast becoming a popular instructional model to guide and support student work, and it is well suited for performance assessment and competency credits. There are many DT models. In one, using the acronym LAUNCH, students begin by "looking, listening, learning," then "ask tons of questions" in order to "understand a process or problem." With a problem found and defined, students need to ideate solutions to generate many options and "navigate" amongst those ideas to help them determine what prototype to "create." Students move the project toward completion by "highlighting" weaknesses identified in the prototype and fixing them before "launching" to a real-world audience (Spencer & Juliani, 2016).

C. Portfolios and Student Work Products

Digital portfolios will increasingly serve competency-based crediting in a variety of ways. As noted in the introduction, the relatively new availability of electronic platforms to host and organize demonstrated competencies is one of the things making this transformation so timely.

Portfolios can be categorized in CBC in two ways: one relatively simple, one considerably more complex and elaborated.

models, students take courses, or undertake experiences inside school, and then complete the course or the experience with a robust performance task. The task—be it an extended essay, a short film, a public presentation, a model, a computer program, a student-designed laboratory experiment—is assessed for competency or mastery. When certified for competency, the evidence of this performance can and should then be inserted into the student portfolio. Portfolios sometimes suffer for lack of consistent, continuous, and effectively assessed content. When only archiving an expansive collection of essays, routine lab reports, or Powerpoint presentations, they lack luster, and the energy required to sustain them can fade. But as CBC grows to entail more demanding and extended tasks, portfolios perhaps can become consequently more dynamic, informative, and engaging.

Portfolios that effectively capture and efficiently display the quality of student work may generate greater confidence in the quality of the new CBC system, something especially important because of the understandable skepticism that competency-based education may provoke. The longtime and esteemed leader of American Association of Colleges and Universities (AAC&U) Carol Geary Schneider writes:

> Educators also need to look with a high degree of skepticism at so-called innovative programs that claim the language of "competency" but in fact have simply slapped new labels on certifiably under-performing practices borrowed from traditional higher education.
>
> (Schneider, 2017)

The title of Schneider's article is "the Proof is in the Portfolio." In it, she discusses several key concerns and complaints about the true quality of competency-based crediting models, some of which correspond to what has been written earlier about the shortfalls, real and perceived, of the Western Governors University model and the NCEA in New Zealand. She then proclaims that the only way for competency-based advocates to overcome criticism is to show the evidence that students have attained deep understanding and can perform transfer masterfully.

> Ultimately, we need to evaluate the "transformative claims" made for specific innovations against the evidence of student competency that is—or is not—transparently demonstrated in students'

own portfolios of educational accomplishments. The proof about students' competency development should be found in their actual work. A competency design for an entire program is a good beginning. But students themselves need to show us what they can do with their learning.

(Schneider, 2017)

Complex

The portfolios become more complex when they entail the kinds of tagging, sorting, and reflections used by the Lerner Medical College and intended by the MTC. As noted, these more powerful platforms entail a sophisticated flowchart and employ significant algorithmic power demanded to fulfill those needs. As Vander Ark notes on his Getting Smart blog, "The Mastery Transcript platform will require a lot of integrations (SIS, LMS, portfolio)" (Vander Ark, 2017). He refers to the need to ensure that whatever platform a portfolio sits on, and especially as it becomes more elaborate, it will need to "play nice" with the many other electronic tools and files schools and systems employ such as student information systems (SIS) and Learning Management Systems (LMS).

Portfolio systems, when well implemented by skillful educators, offer the additional advantage of providing a vehicle for enhanced formative assessment. The very process, when well structured, of students entering evidence, generating reflections, and then submitting that work for review and feedback in a dynamic and iterative way, can powerfully aid students in improving their skills and knowledge. Recall that at Lerner Medical College, student portfolios were designed with an equal attention to formative assessment. "A major goal of repetitive cycles of self-assessment and reflection with close mentoring by advisors is to develop the students' habits of reflective practice" (Dannefer & Henson, 2007).

Portfolios often prove much harder to manage than they might appear. Educators should place a high priority on seeking a portfolio platform that is easy for all to use, intuitive, and puts the student's finished work in the most flattering light, showcased for the viewer.

It isn't the technical features that make the greatest difference in defining success for portfolios; it's the quality of the work. Quality doesn't derive exclusively from student talent and motivation, nor from the excellence of instruction: it is highly influenced by school culture, norms, and protocols.

Ron Berger, author of the seminal book *An Ethic of Excellence: Building a Culture of Craftsmanship with Students*, has thought about this topic at greater length and more deeply than most others. Berger is himself a cabinetmaker by trade, in addition to being an elementary educator and instructional designer, and he uses fine carpentry as an extended metaphor for student workmanship. As he writes, craftsmanship "connotes someone who has integrity, knowledge, dedication, and pride in work—someone who thinks carefully and does things well" (Berger, 2003).

Berger offers five strategies for educators to use to create these craftsmanship cultures; these aren't one-time shortcuts, but rather embedded school norms that best begin in elementary school and are consistently sustained throughout a student's career to achieve the maximum impact.

1. Assign work that matters. Students need assignments that challenge and inspire them.
2. Study examples of excellence. Before they begin work on a project, the teacher and students examine models of excellence—high-quality work done by previous students as well as work done by professionals.
3. Build a culture of critique. Formal critique sessions build a culture of critique that is essential for improving students' work. The rules for group critique: "Be kind; be specific; be helpful."
4. Require multiple revisions. In most schools, students turn in first drafts—work that doesn't represent their best effort and that is typically discarded after it has been graded and returned. In life, when the quality of one's work really matters, one almost never submits a first draft. An ethic of excellence requires revision.
5. Provide opportunities for public presentation. Every final draft students complete is done for an outside audience—whether a class of kindergartners, the principal, or the wider community. The teacher's role is not as the sole judge of their work but rather similar to that of a sports coach or play director—helping them get their work ready for the public eye.

(Berger, 2006)

D. Assessing Performance with Rubrics

Bob Lenz, who founded Envision Schools in California and now directs the Buck Institute for Education, wrote in the book *Transforming Schools*:

Over the last twenty years, the tool that has gained widespread acceptance for meeting the challenge of defining and determining "mastery" is the rubric, whose defining characteristic is its insistence on words, rather than abstract symbols, to describe the quality of the work.

(Lenz, Wells, & Kingston, 2015)

As we've seen, assessment of mastery demands rich and robust student "performances" in which students must transfer skill and understanding to a novel and challenging task. Rubrics are required, nearly always, for evaluating the quality of such performances. Where no judgment is required, rubrics offer no assistance. Multiple-choice tests, or other similar formats in which there is a specific and certain right and wrong answer (fill in the blank, T/F, etc.), don't call for rubrics. But the converse is also true: tasks that have no specific or single right answer, that require judgment to assess, nearly always benefit from the use of rubrics.

Rubrics have additional advantages. They greatly clarify for students (and parents) what the learning targets are for any given task, and thus help students direct efforts to what is most important. They also clarify for teachers what the learning targets are for any given task. As Lenz has written, "It's not the form of the tool that gives rubrics their power. It is the practices—the thinking and actions—that surround rubrics that have made them a transformative force in education" (Lenz, Wells, & Kingston, 2015).

Rubrics are demonstrably more accurate than conventional letter/numerical grading. In a study cited by Marzano, letter grades assigned without rubrics by teachers for student work had correlations to external tests of the same content of 0.42 for Social Studies, 0.44 for Math, 0.50 for Reading, and 0.58 for Language arts. By contrast, rubric-generated grades had correlations better by 0.12 to 0.27 points: 0.57 for Social Studies; 0.71 for Math; 0.71 for Reading; 0.70 for Language Arts, where correlation is determined on a 0–1.0 scale, with 1.0 a "perfect" correlation (Marzano, 2006).

Teachers and administrators widely misunderstand rubrics. This author visits classrooms frequently, and finds many teachers using grading "checklists" mistakenly described as rubrics. In a checklist, the teacher simply states a series of requirements, many of them perfunctory or unattached to the high-priority learning objectives, and awards points to students for correctly following formatting directions or including certain content in a task.

An effective rubric provides students with clear and concrete understandings of their specific proficiency levels in each of a set of several high-priority intended outcomes (understandings and skills, i.e. standards), the criteria for that assignment, and/or for the course, department, division, and/or school.

Designing Rubrics

Analytic rubrics break what is to be assessed into several components to be assessed separately. Educators should design analytic rubrics as two-dimensional tables with three to six rows and columns. For assessing a competency, the rows are used to break down that competency into its key elements, ensuring that nothing important is left out and that extraneous, noncritical components are not added. Generally these rows contain what are called the criteria for what is being assessed. Criteria are usually best capped at six so as to not overburden the cognitive load during assessment (Martin, 2018).

Using consistent criteria over the course of a semester or longer helps students become that much more familiar with, and perhaps internalize, the key things they are intended to develop and master. As Lenz explains:

> For communication to be more effective, a rubric should be used both before the performance and after. The same rubric should be used across multiple performances, offering many chances to meet one clearly articulated set of expectations. Mastering a skill comes not only through practice but also through a deepening understanding of the expectations. The more opportunities, the better. The benefits of a rubric's repeated use within one course only compound when the rubric is used across multiple courses and years.
>
> (Lenz, Wells, & Kingston, 2015)

Using consistent criteria also makes teachers' work easier, because the teachers can become that much more skillful in applying the criteria. Doing so also allows teachers to track student and class progress over the breadth of a semester. If a student displays, or a class of students displays, only a low proficiency level on a particular criterion, teachers can highlight that intended learning in their teaching and reassess it multiple times to ensure that the student grows accordingly (Martin, 2018).

Use vertical columns to define and distinguish proficiency levels. Often these begin on the left with the lowest level, and then proceed left to right from a low-level proficiency to a high-level one. Most often rubrics describe between three and six levels. Offering too few levels limits the rubrics' ability to communicate the students' specific level of skill at a given time in their learning process, and thereby reduce students' ability to self-monitor and advance their proficiency. Too little information on proficiency leaves students wondering why they received the grade they did or, in a nongraded mastery system, limits their opportunity to know how to improve their performance if they haven't yet demonstrated proficiency and earned their credits (Martin, 2018).

Too many proficiency levels can also be problematic, because rarely can skill levels in a particular criterion be meaningfully distinguished in more than four, five, or six levels of performance.. As Susan Brookhart summarizes in her book, *How to Create and Use Rubrics for Formative Assessment and Grading*, "use as many levels as you can describe in terms of meaningful differences in performance quality" (Brookhart, 2013).

Effectively describing and differentiating proficiency levels in ways that students and colleagues can easily and consistently understand is challenging. Many rubric-writers make the mistake of opting for the easy way out, using evaluative or judgmental terms in writing about each level. The problem is that, while the rubric-writer may know the difference between what is excellent, good, fair, and poor, students don't. The problem is not just for students. When seeking to establish inter-rater reliability for rubrics, such that different teachers or assessors can use the same rubric to consistently grade student work, evaluative, rather than descriptive, language fails to provide this reliability because different graders will understand labels like "good" versus "excellent," or "frequently" versus "occasionally," very differently (Martin, 2018).

This "descriptive not evaluative language" concept is subtle and sometimes requires some extended consideration. For example, a rubric designer might state that highly proficient writing is marked by rhetoric that is "compelling to the reader and very persuasive." But students don't know already what makes for compelling or persuasive writing, and colleagues might have a different set of associations with these terms. Instead, consider writing something to the effect that highly proficient rhetoric entails "vivid and specific anecdotes that are of particular or personal interest to the intended reader, and supported by a set of data points arranged and introduced to provide a substantial compilation of evidence for the case being made" (Martin, 2018).

There is also growing enthusiasm for so-called "one-point rubrics." In this format, the specific criterion being assessed is stated in just a single form, that of proficiency, and assessors mark that criterion as met or unmet, and then might provide additional commentary. This approach certainly has advantages, and might be particularly suited for competency-based crediting assessment that is ungraded and focused on the binary determination of mastery or not. On the website Edutopia, an educator named Danah Hashem has laid out several advantages to doing so. One-point rubrics reduce "students' tendency to rank themselves and to compare themselves to or compete with one another . . . helps take student attention off the grade . . . creates more flexibility without sacrificing clarity . . . [and is] simple" (Hashem, 2017).

When rubrics are used for stakes—to determine whether a student has demonstrated mastery and earned a credit for a competency, for instance—rubric design should be carefully planned and developed in a collegial, collaborative process. Teachers and other assessors should be trained in their design, and should follow school or system guidelines that adhere to specific parameters. Drafted rubrics should be ushered through a deliberative process in which administrators or expert panelists review and provide feedback for that rubric before teachers can deploy them for stakes.

Designing rubrics well is only step one in their effective implementation and deployment. Schools and systems also need to ensure they are used consistently and effectively, with strong inter-rater reliability. When the same rubric is used by different teachers and assessors for the same student performance or task, is the assessment rating that results the same or, at minimum, very similar? If not, the system isn't awarding competency credits fairly, and, before long, the system will lose credibility and authority in the eyes of students, parents, and others.

Advancing toward inter-rater reliability isn't a terribly complicated process, but it requires discipline. Ideally, before a high stakes rubric is used for awarding credits, it should be practiced against sample student work products. If this isn't possible, then it should be tested in the first few rounds of its application. A group of assessors—three to five, perhaps a few more—should take the time to compare their individual ratings and check for variance. The expectation of perfect consistency cannot be set too high; this is a human process of evaluation and will always entail some degree of diversity. But if when using a five-point scale (five different performance levels), there's more than a one-point differential on any individual criterion or if there's more than 25% outlier ratings on even a single criterion, that criterion rating scale deserves to be reviewed. Outliers should explain their reasoning. The group should determine whether to accept the alternative perspective or refute it, and should decide whether the scale itself needs revising to reduce the possibility of that differing interpretation. The process should repeat itself several times until ratings come into greater consistency.

Rubric reliability is not easy to come by. Readers will recall that the Lerner Medical College faculty expended a great deal of energy and attention to arrive at greater consistency in their use of rubrics.

Assessment and rubric reliability is only half the battle. Of additional importance is assessment validity. As educators ask others, and especially as they ask university admission officers, to treat these new records of student competency with respect and credibility, they ought take seriously the work of validating competencies with external indicators.

In a report entitled *Measuring Mastery*, authors McClarty and Gaertner write, "External validity evidence is critical to supporting the claim that competency-based education (CBE) programs can make about the relationship between their measures of competence and . . . [future] success." Although writing about higher education competency-based systems, such as that at Western Governors University, the recommendations they make are pertinent to K-12 CBE as well (McClarty & Gaertner, 2015).

External validity can be determined by concurrent validity evidence, or predictive validity evidence. Concurrent evidence is found after comparing "assessment results with other measures collected concurrently" (McClarty & Gaertner, 2015). Student performance internally assessed should be compared, when possible, to external assessments of the same competencies. Do students who earn more Quantitative Analysis credits score higher on the ACT, or pass AP Calculus exams at a higher rate? Do students who earn, or earn more, critical thinking and analytic reasoning competency credits score higher on the College Work Readiness Assessment (CWRA)? Do students who earn persistence credits score higher on the ACT Tessera grit assessment?

"Predictive validity is critical when assessment scores will be used to predict a future outcome." Just as an AP test is deemed valid when students with higher AP scores in high school perform better in related college coursework, so competency credits can be validated with a study of grades in related college coursework after graduation. The report also explains how to use an expanded validity analysis, including defining relevant outcomes for each competency, designing appropriate studies, conducting studies and synthesizing results, reviewing and monitoring, to determine appropriate thresholds or cut scores for determining proficiency or mastery (McClarty & Gaertner, 2015).

As the authors of this report note, "We hope that as years pass and CBE programs mature, more institutions undertake and publish rigorous validity studies to establish a research base commensurate with CBE's growing popularity" (McClarty & Gaertner, 2015).

Resources for High Quality Rubrics

There are many resources available for high-quality rubrics, which, in some cases, can be copied and pasted verbatim, modified, or used as models or inspirations.

A. ACT, the organization best known for its college admission test, has published a sweeping and comprehensive research product called the Holistic Framework, containing the four domains that have been very well established as necessary for success in college and careers. The Holistic Framework domains include the very familiar core academic skills in English Language, Arts, Math, and Science, and also in cross-cutting competencies such as critical thinking, and in Behavioral Skills and Career/Navigation aptitudes. At an open online site found at www.frameworks.act.org, readers can find each domain broken out into many specific and detailed components, subcomponents, and skills. Each skill area is then developmentally differentiated for different grade groupings, including one for middle school and one for high school, and for each of these, a rubric is provided that defines student performance at highly effective, effective, somewhat effective, and not effective levels. These rubrics will not usually stand alone for the purposes of assessing competencies, but can be used helpfully to inform or enhance competency credits (Camara, et al., 2015).

B. The Buck Institute of Education, the leading professional resource for Project-based learning (PBL) in K-12, has many rubrics posted on their website for use in PBL and beyond. Among its freely downloadable rubrics are ones for Collaboration, Presentation, and Creativity and Innovation. The Buck Institute of Education also provides a very useful "Rubric for Rubrics" with which educators can evaluate the quality of the rubrics they design locally (Rubrics-Buck Institute of Education, n.d.).

C. The AAC&U has published a set of rubrics. The VALUE (Valid Assessment of Learning in Undergraduate Education) rubrics include Inquiry and Analysis; Critical Thinking; Creative Thinking; Written Communication; Oral Communication; Quantitative Literacy; Information Literacy; Reading; Teamwork; Problem-Solving; Civic Knowledge and Engagement—Local and Global; Intercultural Knowledge and Competence; Ethical Reasoning and Action; Global Learning; Foundations and Skills for Lifelong Learning; and Integrative Learning. These rubrics, having been written for college students, might be of particular interest and value at college preparatory secondary schools (Association of American Colleges and Universities, 2009).

D. For Mathematics, NCTM (the National Council of Teachers of Mathematics) provides its members something they call EMRF: Everyday Rubric Grading, "a rubric grading system that incorporates the NCTM assessment standards." It includes a "process for writing rubrics that define[s] expectations for student work and helps teachers create an open, equitable, student-centered grading process" (Stutzman & Race, 2004).

E. For English teachers, Education Northwest provides widely respected Six Plus One rubrics for use for K-12 writing assignments. "The rubrics are field tested, research-based, and teacher friendly. The latest versions are designed for easier use across text types (i.e., informative/explanatory, argument, and narrative writing)" (Jones, 2014).

F. For Science, Social Studies, and Foreign Language teachers, the NSTA (National Science Teachers Association), NCSS (National Council for the Social Studies), and ACTFL (American Council on the Teaching of Foreign Languages) offer a number of resources on the use of rubrics in the science classroom. Type in rubrics into their website search boxes to find out more.

G. Catalina Foothills School District in Arizona has published rubrics for Lifelong learners (Catalina Foothills School District, n.d.).

E. Transcripts

Carefully defined competencies, student learning experience, portfolios of work products, and rubric-guided assessments must now flow into and be coherently organized into something that is so much more than a static piece of paper or pdf, so much more than the simple, single document that lists the courses taken and their associated credits and grades. The resulting product, however, must be received, read, scanned, absorbed, and integrated within a college admission office (or employer hiring department) for consideration and decision-making; it must be shaped in such a way, appropriately squared and sized, that it can be effectively plugged into the socket that transcript receivers have long relied on.

This new product must still be a "transcript" as we know the term. This is a fundamental challenge, perhaps the greatest of many, to the work of creating and widely distributing what we are calling competency-based crediting. For many reasons, educators are seeking ways to collect, curate, and convey a vastly wider picture, one so much more detailed, differentiated, diverse, and evidence-based than we have ever had before that to call it a transcript sells it far too short.

But the transcript receivers aren't necessarily receptive to this innovation. Like it or not, schools are obligated to ensure receivers can use and systematize what is provided to them.

The options are twofold: start now with a simple transcript format that refuses to let the perfect be the enemy of the good, or wait for high-powered, technologically supported solutions.

Start Small and Simple

Transcripts in New Zealand just list credits earned for competency standards in a traditional-looking list format, published online. New Zealand's colleges and universities are familiar with the national ministry's format, but Kiwi students apply to and enroll in colleges and universities around the world, and those global institutions have managed to learn how to read and use this format, so there must be at least a small amount of familiarity with this type of school record.

Schools could also add to this "simple" transcript links to their published competency statements, rigorous rubrics, and portfolios of student work.

Many schools may find they need to organize and package competency credits into conventional course groupings, use a formula to convert mastery assessment to letter grades, and send along these alternate forms in a dual transcript submission. These schools should do so with the hope and understanding that this is just an interim phase of a fuller transition.

Wait for Technology Solutions

Alternatively, schools can await the forthcoming tech solutions underway from many organizations, including the Mastery Transcript Consortium and a variety of other national and international projects.

This is not a problem unique to secondary school education by any means; many organizations are grappling with it and are seeking solutions to reconcile the competing tensions of conveying student competencies more thoroughly to institutions that are limited in their means of processing their complexity. IMS Global, for instance, frames the problem this way:

> Skill gaps and mismatches are resulting in missed employment opportunities for learners young and old. Institutions' competency-based learning programs are increasingly designed to focus on the needed skills. But scalable digital communication of a learner's verified knowledge, skills and abilities remains a problem to be solved.
>
> (IMS Global Learning Consortium, Inc., 2017)

In a video posted on the IMS Global site, Jon Mott, Chief Learning Officer at a company called Learning Objects, advocates for an IMS project in which a transcript can truly capture the myriad ways young people, or really people of any age, can be fairly and effectively recognized and credited for their competencies, regardless of where that learning happens (Mott, 2016). IMS describes this as a way in which:

> Members, collaborating with members of the Competency-Based Education Network, the American Association of Registrars and Academic Officers and National Association of Student Personnel Administrators design a new digital achievements record called eT, for extended transcript. The eT achievement record complements credentialing validation efforts such as the Credentials Engine while filling a critical need for learning organization data standards.
>
> (IMS Global Learning Consortium, Inc., 2017)

Fully functional, high-quality, universally accepted and appreciated, and comprehensive transcripts are already underway and yet will be a long time coming. It can be expected that there will be much "versioning," that each newly arriving release will excite some and dismay others, that there will be a dynamic period of experimentation and disequilibrium before we arrive at a new synthesis. The destination, however, should redeem the ride.

References

Amidon, J., Monroe, A., & Ortwein, M. (n.d.). Planning & Teaching Strategies. Retrieved September 17, 2018, from https://courses.lumenlearning.com/educationx92x1/chapter/webbs-depth-of-knowledge/

Association of American Colleges and Universities (2009). VALUE Rubrics. Retrieved from www.aacu.org/value-rubrics

Bassett, P. F. (2009, Fall). *Demonstrations of Learning for 21st-Century Schools.* Online: NAIS. www.nais.org/magazine/independent-school/fall-2009/demonstrations-of-learning-for-21st-century-school/

Berger, R. (2003). *An Ethic of Excellence: Building a Culture of Craftsmanship with Students.* Portsmouth, NH: Heinemann.

Berger, R. (2006). Fostering an Ethic of Excellence. *The Fourth and Fifth Rs,* 12(1), Fall/Winter 2006.

Brookhart, S. M. (2013). *How to Create and Use Rubrics for Formative Assessment and Grading.* Alexandria, VA: ASCD.

Camara, W., O'Connor, R., Mattern, K., & Hanson, M. A., Eds. (2015). *Beyond Academics: A Holistic Framework for Enhancing Education and Workplace Success.* ACT Research Report Series. Iowa City, IA: ACT.

Catalina Foothills School District (n.d.). Resources for Deep Learning. Retrieved September 17, 2018, from www.cfsd16.org/index.php/academics/resources-for-deep-learning

Colby, R. (2017). *Competency-Based Education: A New Architecture for K-12 Schooling.* Cambridge, MA: Harvard Education Press.

Dannefer, E. F. & Henson, L. C. (2007). The Portfolio Approach to Competency-Based Assessment at the Cleveland Clinic Lerner College of Medicine. *Academic Medicine,* 82(5), 493–502. doi:10.1097/acm.0b013e31803ead30

Hashem, D. (2017, October 24). 6 Reasons to Try a Single-Point Rubric. Retrieved September 17, 2018, from www.edutopia.org/article/6-reasons-try-single-point-rubric

Henry County (GA) Schools (n.d.). *Competency-Based Learning in Social Studies.* Online: Blackboard. https://schoolwires.henry.k12.ga.us/Page/90011

Hess, K. J. (2018). *A Local Assessment Toolkit to Promote Deeper Learning: Transforming Research Into Practice.* Thousand Oaks, CA: Corwin.

Hewlett Foundation (2013). *Deeper Learning Defined.* Online: Hewlett. www.hewlett. org/library/deeper-learning-defined/

IMS Global Learning Consortium, Inc. (2017). *Extended Transcript Phase II Achievements Records Standard and Skills Center Search* (Report).

ISTE (2007). *ISTE Standards: Students.* Online: ISTE. www.iste.org/docs/pdfs/20-14_ISTE_Standards-S_PDF.pdf

Jones, J. (2014, October 6). 6+1 Trait® Rubrics. Retrieved September 17, 2018, from http://educationnorthwest.org/traits/traits-rubrics

Lenz, B., Wells, J., & Kingston, S. (2015). *Transforming Schools: Using Project-Based Learning, Performance Assessment, and Common Core Standards.* San Francisco, CA: Jossey-Bass.

Martin, J. (2018). *Enhancing Student Learning and Grading with Rubrics* (Report). Charleston, SC: Blackbaud.

McClarty, K. & Gaertner, M. (2015). *Measuring Mastery: Best Practices for Assessment in Competency-Based Education* (Report). Washington, DC: Center on Higher Education Reform American Enterprise Institute.

McTighe, J. (2013). *Designing Cornerstone Tasks to Promote Meaningful Learning and Assess What Matters Most.* Unpublished document.

Mott, J. (2016, May 27). Empowering and Enabling Learners (Video file). Retrieved September 17, 2018, from www.youtube.com/watch?v=iKeA7NI uMtE&feature=youtu.be

NAIS (National Association of Independent Schools) (2010). *Essential Capacities for the 21st Century* (Report). Schools of the Future Committee, NAIS Commission on Accreditation.

NCTE (2012). *NCTE/IRA Standards for the English Language Arts, Standard #6.* Online: NCTE. www.ncte.org/standards/ncte-ira

New Hampshire Department of Education (2012). *State Model Competencies.* Online: New Hampshire Dept. of Education. www.education.nh.gov/innovations/ hs_redesign/competencies.htm

NGSS (n.d.). Online: Next Generation Science Standards. www.nextgenscience.org

NHDOE for NH State Board of Education (2010). FINAL: Course Level Competency Validation Rubric.

Niguidula, D. A. (2019). *Demonstrating Student Mastery with Digital Badges and Portfolios.* Alexandria, VA: ASCD.

OECD (2013). *PISA 2012 Assessment and Analytical Framework: Mathematics, Reading, Science, Problem Solving and Financial Literacy.* Paris: OECD Publishing. http://dx.doi. org/10.1787/9789264190511-en

Partnership for 21st Century Skills (2009). *Standards: A 21st Century Skills Implementation Guide.* Online: Partnership for 21st Century Skills. www.p21.org/storage/ documents/p21-stateimp_standards.pdf

Rubrics-Buck Institute of Education (n.d.). Retrieved September 17, 2018, from www.bie.org/objects/cat/rubrics

Schaef, S. (2016, October 9). What IS the Difference Between Competencies and Standards? [Web log post]. Retrieved September 16, 2018, from www. redesignu.org/what-difference-between-competencies-and-standards

Schneider, C. G. (2017, April 1). The Proof is in the Portfolio. Retrieved September 17, 2018, from www.aacu.org/publications-research/periodicals/proof-portfolio

Spencer, J. & Juliani, A. J. (2016). *Launch: Using Design Thinking to Boost Creativity and Bring Out the Maker in Every Student*. San Diego, CA: Dave Burgess Consulting.

Stutzman, R. & Race, K. (2004, January). EMRF: Everyday Rubric Grading. Retrieved September 17, 2018, from www.nctm.org/Publications/mathematics-teacher/2004/Vol97/Issue1/EMRF_-Everyday-Rubric-Grading/

Vander Ark, T. (2017, September 14). School Consortium Proposes a Better Transcript. Retrieved September 17, 2018, from www.gettingsmart.com/2017/09/school-consortium-proposes-a-better-transcript/

Wiggins, G. P. "Teaching to the Authentic Test." *Educational Leadership*, 46(7), 41–47 Apr 1989.

Wiggins G. P. & McTighe, J. (2008). *Understanding by Design*. Alexandria, VA: Association for Supervision and Curriculum Development.

5

Downstream Effects on Schools and Systems, Curriculum, and Instruction

Competency-based crediting should have a far-reaching, transformative impact on schools and school systems, curriculum, and instruction. Where, when, and how students are credited for their learning will all change, and the role of the teacher will change. Although it is impossible to be exhaustive or entirely accurate in determining these implications, it is feasible to consider some of the major likely or possible implications of this shift.

A caveat: although the following effects are plausible results "downstream," few are certain or inevitable. It's not hard to envision scenarios by which many schools and systems change the container and not the contents. Conventional schooling patterns exert powerful influence, and some school transformative efforts may be co-opted by the traditionalists, who sign on to the new way of crediting students without changing their day-to-day practices much at all. In the discussion of New Zealand's NCEA in a previous chapter, we discussed how widely this "co-opting" occurred in that nation following the adoption a dramatically different kind of transcript and student learning crediting system. While those seeking broad educational transformation in New Zealand have been disappointed, the new system has nonetheless unleashed in some schools genuinely inspiring change: the difference has been in the leadership and the execution of this change.

Let's look at the three major implications for schooling in each of three domains: schools and school systems, curriculum, and instruction.

Schools and School Systems

Stamp Schooling with School-Specific Values

With competency-based crediting, schools and school systems (abbreviated hereafter to schools) will better be able to design and deliver learning that reflects their particular values and their aspirations for students and that is more suited to the needs of their region and student demographics. This will also enable schools to differentiate themselves one from another, allowing more meaningful choice for students and families.

Today there are many schools that seek to distinguish their programs through particular intended outcomes. New Tech Network schools have declared collaboration and agency to be two signature emphases in their students' preparation. Other schools highlight social justice, community engagement, creative problem-solving, and technological proficiency among their defining attributes. However, at present, these schools have only limited leeway to map these intended outcomes onto their student learning because of the limitations of the current curriculum tied to classes and courses in semester- or year-long blocks, awarding credits only for the completion of the seat time in those courses. The shift this book foresees will eliminate the obstacles that the current system poses. As an example of this potential, look again to the marvelous example of the unique and culturally responsive teaching and learning that New Zealand's NCEA has made possible for the students of Kia Aroha College.

Stepping Forward

Determine and Deploy School-Specific "Demonstrations of Learning"

About a decade ago, the National Association of Independent Schools' then-president Pat Bassett wrote an article entitled "Demonstrations of Learning for 21st-Century Schools," arguing that "if we could agree on what well-educated students should be able to do, teachers, schools, and systems could then "backward design" the means to those ends." In Bassett's view, schools could each define their own list, reflecting their own mission, history and philosophy, or what students should be able to do; prepare students, record their completion, and present graduates to the next institution with those distinct and masterful skill sets.

Bassett suggested as examples things like:

- Construct and program a robot capable of performing a difficult physical task;
- Using statistics, assess whether or not a statement by a public figure is demonstrably true;
- Assess media coverage of a global event from various cultural/ national perspectives; and
- Describe a breakthrough for a team on which you served and to which you contributed to overcoming a human-created obstacle so that the team could succeed in its task.

Competency-based crediting empowers schools to make their demonstrations of learning fully embedded in the schooling of their students (Bassett, 2009).

Expand Where Schooling Happens

There's nothing new about "schools without walls" of course, but CBC will allow schools to greatly broaden this type of learning and crediting. Schools can welcome and encourage students to go outside their building and learn in the public library, the nearby university, the software startup down the street, or the congresswoman's office downtown—and can effectively credit students for that learning. Over time, this will require schools to rethink the way their schedules work, the way their facilities are designed, and the way they participate in public transportation and partner with community organizations.

Stepping Forward

Build a Database of Community Connections

As part of a summer registration process, ask parents to complete a few survey questions about their current (and perhaps past) places of work and organizations which which they have strong affiliations—and ask them to indicate if they are in a position to make introductions or arrange student activities. Survey your alumni and other community partners in a similar way. Organize survey results into an easy-to-use database, and train teachers and counselors on its use.

Look also for whether there might be a wider community database for this purpose in your school district office, at the United Way, or in some local project dedicated to this kind of school-workplace-community synergy. Tucson, Arizona, is home to such an operation, called Community Share; it describes itself as a "locally based online network that connects the skills and experiences of passionate community partners—individual professionals, community leaders, organizations and businesses—in the greater Tucson region with the goals and needs of educators in schools and informal learning environments." Your community doesn't have a Community Share equivalent? Tap your network and work to launch one.

Appoint a Staff or Volunteer for Community Outreach

High Tech High campuses in San Diego often include on their staffs full- or part-time administrators with the dedicated role of community outreach and partnerships. These critical people attend community meetings and events, network through every channel available to them, and generate opportunities for work-site and place-based learning. Many schools won't be able to fund such a position, but this could be a great way to engage volunteer parents or senior citizens looking for meaningful ways to participate in and contribute to your students' schooling.

Expand Who Students Are

It is possible to consider even further decoupling from our traditional notions of what a school is. MTC founder and Board Chair Scott Looney has speculated that there might be a change in the very notion of who might be included in a school's student population. (Looney, 2016) Once a school has defined its unique set of competencies and built an assessment system and panel to evaluate student work and award credits for demonstrating mastery in those competencies, why couldn't that school welcome students from any location, students who have never set foot in a school classroom, to submit work products for consideration, evaluation, credit, and ultimately diploma? This scenario is probably more distant than the others, but it might help educators reflect on the depth and breadth of the way competency crediting can change schooling.

Stepping Forward

Establish "Sister School" and Arrange Credit Swaps

Many schools already have sister schools—sometimes internationally—with which they do exchanges: sometimes in a particular kind of schooling network in which they participate; sometimes in a public-private school partnership collaboration. What would it take to enroll a student, virtually if long-distance and physically if nearby, into a high school credit-bearing class, and award them that credit. As you shift toward defining credits for competency, experimenting with this and defining some primarily by their demonstration, not their "seat-time," how could you offer up that demonstration evaluation—and credit-awarding—opportunity to sister school students? Surely some international students would thrill to that opportunity to include credits from a recognized and accredited US school if applying to US universities.

Have connections in New Zealand? Think about the learning opportunity for your school to partner with a school there for a mutual arrangement of offering competency-based credits. (See the discussion of New Zealand practices in Chapter 2.)

Curriculum

Curriculum Becomes More Discrete, Granular, and Modularized

Subject-specific courses, be they in semester- or year-long units, are simply too large, too bulky, for efficiently organizing and documenting learning. Too many different things are contained in a two- or three-word phrase like Algebra 2, English 10, or United States History. A student who attends and brilliantly performs for twelve weeks of a fifteen-week semester but then gets ill and can't complete the final three weeks earns no credit at all, in most cases. Competency crediting will bring about a modularized curriculum broken into more manageable, coherent, and transparent chunks of learning. Some modules will continue to be sequenced in a logical progression, but many of them will become less sequential providing greater flexibility in scheduling.

Stepping Forward

Expand Your Offering of Special Coursework for Partial Credits, and Tie Them to Outcomes

Westminster School in Atlanta has recently implemented a three-week "Jan-term" between semesters, and awards a half-course credit for its completion, recorded on the transcript. Schools advancing experiential learning in their special terms or during school vacations could do the same, and consider how key subject matter and academic skill crediting could be refashioned this way. There needs be an abundance of caution here. In the era of the "Shopping Mall high school," credits became currency—and cheap currency at that—handed out for answering phones in the school office or for lightweight crafting classes (think "basket-weaving") (Powell, Cohen, & Farrar, 1985). Provide these opportunities, but do so while holding high standards for the competencies defined and evaluated.

Experiment Breaking Up Year-Long Courses

Many high schools are already moving away from year-long credits to semester-only course credits, (and not aggregating points or averaging semesters into a year-long grade.) Experiment, for learning and acclimation, splitting up the credits award for a semester-length course, and record credits for their completion individually.

Experiment With Offering Digital Badges

Working with a volunteer set of teachers, design a small set of prototype "badges" that can be awarded for demonstrated academic and and non-academic proficiencies. These can be attached by links from transcripts and referred to in counselor letters to motivate student effort. The digital portfolio platform Richer Picture provides a great vehicle getting started with badging.

Curriculum Design Becomes More Outcome-Focused

This is not to say that curriculum today is never designed toward particular learning outcomes. Standards guide and inform educators quite regularly. But it is still the case that, when planning for a year-long course of study in Algebra, History or Biology, educators often default to a coverage mindset, letting the textbook dictate the content, the pace, and the objectives of the curriculum for that course. Once detached from the textbook curriculum, teachers will need to become more creative and open-minded as they set about designing courses of study so that their students can earn credits for discrete, carefully crafted competencies. On the whole, curriculum will become far more closely tied to intended outcomes. Many educators could benefit from a system that affords them the clarity, direction, and scaffolding that competency crediting would provide.

That said, educators at every level will need to take care not to collapse the experience of inquiry, deliberation, extension, application, and reflection that comprises good learning into a straight-line sprint to the credit course of action that shortchanges students and likely diminishes their lasting understandings and skill proficiencies.

Stepping Forward

Provide Teachers Professional Development in Curriculum Design

In nearly every item on this chapter's list, educators at every level will need to strengthen their own competency to make the shifts required. But this one will probably be the most demanding on classroom teachers, and will entail work far afield from what most learned in education programs. Develop, collaboratively with teachers, a multi-year plan for professional learning in curriculum design. Explore particularly the programs and resources associated with Understanding by Design, authored by Wiggins and McTighe (2008). Programs exist for trainers to come to your school and for teachers to participate in online classes and certificate programs. Place a priority on providing this kind of training.

Visit Model Schools

The shifts in teaching and learning entailed here are not small, and, for many educators, are still quite abstract. Books, articles, and Powerpoint slides can go only so far in building out a full visualized and internalized understanding of this kind of competency-based learning. Field trips for teachers provide valuable immersion in what the future contains for them. Most trailblazing schools welcome visitors and are excited to show off their work and enhance their learning networks. Go visit.

Implement a Competency-Friendly Learning Management System

Too often, online gradebooks and learning management systems are hardwired to support only traditional letter or numeric grading, using conventional units of time or coursework. Reconfiguring them to direct students' attention to competency outcomes, and to assess and credit competencies, can be challenging or impossible. Don't wait: research and select a system that can support a competency-based system early in your process and acquaint your team with how to use it. An exemplary system some schools are quickly adopting for this very purpose is called Motivis Learning. As it explains on its site, "Whether your program is based on credit hours, seat-time, or competencies, it's easy for teachers and faculty to engage with students in a meaningful way" (Learning Relationship Management Platform, n.d.).

Curriculum Becomes More Balanced

In those schools and school systems which choose to align a healthy proportion of their competency credits with "holistic" education, such as social and emotional skills and cross-cutting capacities, the content of the curriculum will follow suit. More time and more resources will become available for students to study, practice, and demonstrate these critical components of a well-rounded education than is almost ever the case currently in a secondary school curriculum devoted to recording achievement only in subject areas.

Stepping Forward

Ensure Goals Align

Review your school or system's statement of educational aims; examine the graduate profile or portrait. Do they include explicit attention to non-cognitive skills? Do they provide greater emphasis and specificity than some half-hearted reference to student character and wellness? Using evidence-based resources like the ACT Holistic Framework, declare a commitment to true whole-child preparation.

Develop Adult Competency

Teachers can't teach well what they don't know and can't do. Promote an adult climate of trust and mutual support, and work to set mutually agreed-upon ground rules for respect and encouragement. Facilitate ways by which educators can self-assess their social and emotional skills, set goals for improvement, and with the support of the school develop over time.

Assess Student Social and Emotional Competencies

One vehicle to elevate attention to the development of these skills in students is by regular assessment. Implement one of the recently developed social-emotional assessment systems, collect data on student skills, and work with the students to set goals and monitor progress. Consider how these assessments could fit into the formation of a set of credits for competency in this arena.

Instruction

Instruction Becomes More Facilitative

Students will need more guidance to determine the appropriate credits to aim toward, and they will benefit from more coaching on an individual and small-group basis in acquiring the learning and developing the skills they need to earn those credits. There will still be times when teachers present whole-class direct instruction; this isn't an absolute pendulum swing from one extreme to the other. But on balance, as students work at different paces and customize their learning, there will be far less need for or value in whole-group direct instruction.

Stepping Forward

Subordinate but Don't Eliminate Lectures

At some New Tech Network schools this author has visited, educators have explained that lectures and presentations by teachers still take place, but in a carefully constructed context whereby they must be sought out and asked for by students. Usually called "workshops," they are provided only "on-demand," upon the explicit request of students. Too often, the lesson planning mindset is to determine first what lessons will be presented, and then student activities are planned to fill in the gaps. The shifts described here require a shift of this mindset too. Plan what students will do first, and what information and skill development they will require to do those things—and then identify how lecturing and presenting can support these needs, in a subordinate role.

Implement or Expand Advisory Programming

Homeroom won't cut it, and counseling (see below) is too often too limited or too distant from students' everyday needs. The shift envisioned entails students being carefully guided step by step to determine, develop, demonstrate, and document a moderately large number of competency credits. Schools can start now by implementing or extending time in the schedule for teacher-student advisory meetings, and supporting greater skill development for teachers in the work of advising.

Expand Role of Counselors and Registrars

US educational systems already suffer from a deeply disturbing lack of counseling, with ratios seeming to rise to newly dizzying heights annually. So this advice is offered with due respect to these fierce limitations. Challenging as it may be, recognize that the work required to transition to competency-based crediting and facilitative instruction is yet more reason to seek and advocate for expanded services from counselors and registrars to guide students through the process. School-leaders: if a change in crediting is coming from state or regional agencies or boards, demand of them the funding for enhanced counseling necessary to fulfill this mandate.

Instruction Becomes More About Designing Learning Experiences

Teachers will increasingly need to embrace their role as learning designers, rather than content deliverers and skills facilitators. What kind of environments and what kind of technology access will students need to be able to work individually and in small groups at different paces or in different directions? What kind of tasks will need to be designed to ensure students can both practice and then demonstrate mastery? As the range of types of competency credit widens to include more holistic elements, teaching too will need to expand in the ability to plan learning these other skills.

Stepping Forward

Embrace Design Thinking Strategies

Design Thinking, as exemplified by the research and practices of Stanford "D-school," can inform a new mindset and method for instruction. Designers recognize the need to understand the problem they are solving, to grapple with the experiences and perspectives of participants in whatever experience or product they are designing, and to prototype and iterate repeatedly until solutions are effective. School leaders should learn more about these practices from book such as *Make Space* (Doorley & Witthoft, 2012) or *Launch* (Spencer & Juliani, 2016), and then explore how to embed this approach more thoroughly in their school—both for the process of curriculum design and for the content of instruction itself.

Change Hiring Practices

Often hiring focuses on the qualifications of the applicants and their ability to stand and deliver in front of a room. These things matter, but they may matter less than the ability to systematically design not just a lesson but a unit—and a course—to ensure that the focus is on what students, not teachers, do. School leaders should ask for applicants to present samples and portfolios of extended instructional design.

Instruction Demands Greater Assessment Competency

Learning in the new crediting system may become more distributed, but assessment becomes more important and more challenging. Students no longer earn credits "just" for 180 days of seat time and an online grade-book calculation of averaged tests and assignments; they are awarded credits for demonstrated mastery of high-level designed competencies entailing transfer and sophisticated thinking. Teachers will need to be highly sophisticated in evaluating complex student work products and in designing and using rubrics to do so.

Stepping Forward

Embed Professional Learning

Professional development for faculty, here as in some of the other items above, is important, but sustained expertise in assessment practice is best developed through structured faculty collaboration in formats exemplified by PLCs—professional learning communities. School leaders should carefully carve out the time for teachers to meet together for a minimum of an hour weekly—preferably more—and use that time following protocols for preparing common assessments and jointly assessing student work. As seen in the discussion in Chapter 2 of Lerner Medical College, it takes many rounds of assessment review and formatted deliberation before educators can reach a new plateau of common methodology and consistent evaluation, and schools would do well to put these systems in place early in their transformation process.

Each of these nine shifts is possible and/or likely has downstream effects, but how thoroughly, and how effectively, they come into fruition depends on the quality of leadership, planning, and professional learning that happens at every level of the educational ecosystem. This shift will likely be truly the singular challenge of a generation of educators (with the potential equally challenging task of promoting genuine equity and inclusion for all students in our schools).

Education schools should consider these implications in the planning of their degree-awarding programs for both teachers and administrators. School boards at every level should review policies and procedures, and consider carefully the implications for school finance, facility planning, staffing, and technology. Educational leaders will need to plan for more and different professional learning, greater technological access for all students, and new forms of professional collaboration.

References

Bassett, P. F. (2009, Fall). *Demonstrations of Learning for 21st-Century Schools.* Online: NAIS. www.nais.org/magazine/independent-school/fall-2009/demonstrations-of-learning-for-21st-century-school/

Doorley, S. & Witthoft, S. (2012). *Make Space: How to Set the Stage for Creative Collaboration.* Hoboken, NJ: John Wiley & Sons.

Learning Relationship Management Platform (n.d.). Retrieved March 6, 2019, from http://motivislearning.com/

Looney, S. (2016, April 28). Mastery Transcript Consortium. Presentation given at Mastery Transcript Consortium Meeting in Cleveland Botanical Garden, Cleveland, Ohio.

Powell, A. G., Cohen, D. K., & Farrar, E. (1985). *The Shopping Mall High School: Winners and Losers in the Educational Marketplace.* Boston, MA: Houghton Mifflin.

Spencer, J. & Juliani, A. J. (2016). *Launch: Using Design Thinking to Boost Creativity and Bring Out the Maker in Every Student.* San Diego, CA: Dave Burgess Consulting.

Wiggins, G. P. & McTighe, J. (2008). *Understanding by Design.* Alexandria, VA: Association for Supervision and Curriculum Development.

6

Learning from Experience

Case Studies of Competency-Based Learning Transformation

Leading schools and school systems through this competency-based crediting and transcript transformation won't be easy. Some educational leaders may find this project the largest and longest exercise of substantial instructional leadership in their entire careers; we can expect and hope that it is also their most consequential and proudest accomplishment. Fortunately, a number of schools and systems have begun this work, and their experiences provide illuminating lessons.

Note that these case studies are not limited to new crediting and transcript models alone, but look more widely at examples of both competency-based education and competency-based crediting shifts.

Alaska

A remarkable story of educational transformation comes from a school district that is among the very largest districts in the nation in area, nearly the size of the state of Virginia, yet serves an enrollment of only about 500 students. These events are chronicled in the fascinating book, Delivering the Promise by Richard DeLorenzo. Alaska's Chugach School District, in 1994, was a failing district in nearly every statistic one could imagine; in the previous twenty years only a single graduate had enrolled in college. Ninety percent of students were below grade level in every assessed area. That year, new leadership arrived, and the transformation began (DeLorenzo, 2009).

All previous incremental efforts to improve performance had gone nowhere. New Superintendent Roger Sampson and new Assistant Superintendent Rich DeLorenzo determined that "change had to happen at the system level." They didn't know what the change would entail, but they did know they needed the kind of people who could handle the challenge, and so they set out to hire people "who were problem-solvers, who were resilient, and who had a moral purpose to serve students" (DeLorenzo, 2009).

Stakeholders were engaged, particularly: the business community, who were asked to define as specifically as possible their concerns and needs from the district; the faculty, to whom "the brutal facts" were fully addressed; and parents, with whom real relationships were developed for the first time. DeLorenzo, deeply curious and a fan of educational research, read widely in Hunter, Maslow, Deming, and Bloom, and brought that research to the work at hand. In 1996, a new vision was declared that included "Basic Skills; School to Life Transition; personal, social, and character development; meeting the individual needs of students; and technology." The vision, though, was relatively the easy part; the next task was creating a set of detailed standards, from scratch, in multiple domains: math, reading, science, social studies, technology, service learning, career development, cultural awareness, and personal/social development (DeLorenzo, 2009).

For each area, the school leadership determined graduate proficiency levels, backward-mapped developmental levels, and began to design aligned assessments for each level. As they did all this hard work, the energetic DeLorenzo encountered educational research expert Robert Marzano's thoughts on a standards-based grading model in which students progressed only upon mastery of each standard. Marzano cautioned that this model "is very difficult to implement because of the massive changes required in scheduling, reporting, and resource association. It is for this reason that no school or district has seriously attempted to implement this model." DeLorenzo happily accepted the challenge. After a half-hearted attempt to manage dual report card systems, letter grades were dropped over some objections, a waiver was sought and received from the state for ending Carnegie unit requirements, and students could only progress and graduate upon demonstrated competency in all ten standards (DeLorenzo, 2009).

Success wasn't immediate. Chugach leadership encountered two major obstacles in their most immediate constituencies, students and parents.

Students expressed enormous resentment at the new expectations and the higher standards, and the leadership realized that, beyond an initial meeting or two, they really hadn't engaged students in any significant way. Redoubling their efforts, they committed themselves to a great deal of listening and explanation to ensure students understood the goals and the structure of the new arrangement. No compromises were made in expectations, but students were given much greater guidance on what they needed to do to meet the new requirements. Some parents had a different concern: without grades, how could they know how their children were performing? Once the assessments were completed and implemented, "parents realized that students would have to prove that they knew the standards" and those concerns were thus alleviated (DeLorenzo, 2009).

The results of this transformation were genuinely spectacular. Reading scores moved from the bottom quartile to the seventy-second percentile nationally; participation in college testing went from 0 to 70%; and the district was awarded the national Malcolm Baldrige award for organizational excellence (DeLorenzo, 2009).

New Zealand

Chapter 2 of this book provides an extensive look at the New Zealand NCEA crediting system, but not how it got there. Richard Wells explains in his book that it "wasn't an easy road to travel . . . make no mistake, the shift required massive effort and commitment . . . . Know that it may take a decade before you see significant progress" (Wells, 2016). In Wells's telling, the new system was introduced in an abrupt manner, and at first most teachers were unprepared to effectively engage with it. Because the education ministry was launching the program to replace a traditional examination system, and because most standards could be assessed with national standardized tests, educators simply viewed the new system as a near replica of the old. At the launch, little communication came from the ministry, and no substantive professional learning was provided. The public was under-informed as to the form or goals of the new system, and the media seized upon examples they encountered of malpractice in administering or assessing the standards. Nevertheless, the ministry stayed the course despite the many hiccups they encountered (Wells, 2016).

Training and communications improved after the "messy" launch, and with the time that the government patiently provided, more and more teachers felt both empowered and confident to experiment within the new parameters. "Moderation" systems have been designed and implemented to ensure that performance tasks and projects are reviewed and signed off by other educators, with best practice entailing moderation from colleagues outside one's own school. To win such approval, proposals must include examples of the kind of evidence that is required. Student work in conventional school courses is awarded credits for meeting standards and is also moderated, both inside the school by colleagues and by a national panel. Finally, the government responded to the national demand from educators for more support by providing a slew of online resources and communities, including a comprehensive information site on the standards, assessments, and student work samples exemplifying each level of performance. Also available is a teacher support site for training, curriculum resources, and connections among educators at every level (Wells, 2016).

California: Bay Area

Nueva School, an independent high school in the San Francisco Bay Area, has used competency-based assessments since its secondary school launched in 2014. Now, it is working toward implementing a mastery transcript and is pushing the project forward through professional development and learning, competency development and review, student engagement, and careful anticipation of obstacles. As it does so, it is working to "revise and improve both the standards, the practice of assessing them, and the architecture of developing a course," according to school administrator Mike Peller (Peller, 2018).

The school has a working group undertaking an ongoing process to develop their competencies, considering questions such as:

1. What do they say about the school's values? (Do they reflect the school's values?)
2. Are they measurable?
3. Do they transfer across disciplines?
4. Are they relevant for the needs of the 21st century?

(Peller, 2018)

One focal point is whether they represent the proper holistic balance, and Peller emphasizes that they take seriously "the research on the importance of non-cognitive skills." As they proceed to determine mastery credits for the competencies, they are also preparing "specific evaluation criteria" for each (Peller, 2018).

Rising twelfth graders are invited "to apply for the opportunity to co-create their transcript," a key step in their engagement with the process. Teachers have been asked to identify the pains and gains of the process for both students and teachers, and leadership is using that input to plan accordingly (Peller, 2018).

Virginia

At Christchurch school in Virginia, educators are eagerly awaiting the arrival of the mastery transcript, and they've been preparing for it for some time. A decade ago, they decided to re-center their curriculum on their specific locale along the Rappahannock river and develop a more connected, interdisciplinary education. First steps included changing the schedule to make room for longer class periods, creating or expanding various interdisciplinary programs such as three-day and one-day travel and field work programs, and offering grade-level projects. However, as Neal Keesee, the school's assistant head, explains in a blog post, they didn't stop issuing letter grades; the faculty felt wedded to them as a motivational tool to ensure student compliance (Keesee, 2017).

The letter grade system for these robust interdisciplinary learning experiences was clunky, however. The work students were doing, and the learning they were acquiring, wasn't easily adding up in the grade book average percentages that the traditional grading system was built to generate. Both because of this clunkiness, and to pave the way toward the mastery transcript, the school is replacing grades for these special programs and projects with narratives. Intended outcomes are still clearly defined with the specific skills students are expected to develop and master in these experiences, and they inform the narrative assessments. The school is also preparing portfolios to host the resulting work products. According to some early indicators, student motivation isn't suffering at all.

> Especially with our older students, we are actually seeing more engagement, as they recognize the effort for greater authenticity. "No grades" alone is not enough—clearly it has to go hand in

hand with authentic instruction, relationships (we are using a small cohort model), some kind of portfolio, and a supportive culture . . . I believe that an official transcript that recognizes student mastery of competencies—recognizes their internally motivated achievement rather than providing a set of external markers—will, over time, change the culture.

(Keesee, 2017)

Vermont

Putney School in Vermont began rethinking the student learning journey in 2012 to determine how best to "put agency into the hands of students, making clear what we want them to know and be able to do, and giving them considerable latitude in how they can reach those goals" (Jones, 2018).

This isn't any abdication of high standards or expectations for students; the school sees it as asking more of students while still providing the necessary supports students need. "Rather than marking the trails through a preset program, we have set clear and ambitious goals and are waiting to see the paths the students find to reach those goals" (Jones, 2018). This is a program launched prior to the Mastery Transcript Consortium, but the Putney Head of School Emily Jones sees the two as complementary. "It's very similar in theory to what the Mastery Transcript Consortium (MTC) schools are working toward—designing better ways to define, teach, and measure the outcomes that the school values" (Jones, 2018).

The process began with an extended series of inquiries: How deeply and consistently does our educational program fulfill its mission, and where are the gaps or inconsistencies? When we assess learning, what is it that we are assessing? What does it really mean to know something, or to be able to do something, and how do we know? Head of School Jones recognizes that these conversations can become traps of intellectual discourse, but recommends them nonetheless.

Facing up to this complexity can be daunting, and each school will have to decide how far down this rabbit hole to venture. If it is avoided entirely, though, a school risks creating a laundry list of academic tasks that will leave some of the fundamental problems unsolved and some of the school's deeply held values unaddressed.

(Jones, 2018)

After contemplating these questions broadly, the leadership turned to the academic departments, asking them to draw up specific documents about their "ideal goals and ambitions—what should students know and be able to do in this discipline?" Jones claims that this exercise helped both to identify common elements across departments, so as to better develop interdisciplinary and coherent school competencies, and to identify those departments less engaged in the process. Those "lagging" groups "wrote wording that essentially paralleled their existing course structure, so as to ensure that nothing in their department would need to change" (Jones, 2018).

The set of outcomes the faculty generated, organized into five categories, was shared and discussed among the school's board of trustees, who appreciated and enjoyed being involved, and added value while fundamentally finding good consensus with the faculty (Jones, 2018).

Many different ways of structuring intended outcomes are available to any school or school system; it is worthwhile to take time to shape them in various ways and test them with various audiences. After thorough consideration, Putney arrived at a three-part structure: "throughlines," for those overarching competencies, the "general skills, aptitudes, and habits of mind," that are found in many disciplines and aspects of learning; "subject-centered objectives;" and "essential experiences" which are fundamental to the school's unique mission and learning program, but not necessarily wrangled into assessments, rubrics, transcripts (Jones, 2018).

This took, in Jones's telling, almost two years. The next phase was focused on rubrics for the throughlines, a full forty-two of them, organized conventionally in four tiers of Novice, Emerging, Proficient, and Beyond, with proficiency serving as the threshold for credit. "Given Putney's progressive bent and insistence on lifelong learning, we avoided any use of the word *mastery*." The rubrics are regularly revisited and revised based on user experience and clarified when confusion occurs (Jones, 2018).

Graduation requirements set a floor of C-level grades, but in these new rubrics, the credit threshold of "proficiency" corresponds more closely to a B. In Jones's view, the school's standards have risen. "Our experience at Putney suggests that the ultimate outcome for many schools—including those that join the efforts of the MTC—will be a higher floor for their graduation requirements" (Jones, 2018).

Outcomes and standards first, rubrics second, portfolios third. With the first two in place, Putney reports working hard on the third, beginning with their ninth graders, the class of 2020. Ninth grade teachers and students worked in an iterative way to try various approaches, forms, and languages in the portfolio, and after finding their way to a workable arrangement, those teachers began training their colleagues. Time is set aside for students to manage this work; they:

> look at the standards and rubrics, choose work to put in their portfolio, and write reflective notes explaining why they believe that piece of work shows what the standard intends . . . For each piece of work they include, the student writes a short explanation of how that work demonstrates a particular learning objective, and there is space for faculty comment. Ultimately they will curate and cull their portfolios to choose the best representations of their learning before graduation.
>
> (Jones, 2018)

Jones writes that the school had made a commitment to not implement changes that would appear likely to hurt college admissions prospects, and pending the completion and proven effectiveness of the Mastery Transcript Consortium, Putney will continue to send colleges "dual transcripts," one of them containing letter grades. They are confident that, despite this temporary compromise, the fuller implementation of their approach and the MTC eventually "will change not only education in the United States and elsewhere, but it will have a lasting impact on creativity, mental health, and our democracy and culture" (Jones, 2018).

> In reflecting upon her school's journey, Jones makes several recommendations. One is patience. It was four years of work, she writes, before they began implementation with the first ninth grade class, and they are continually refining it. We did not make a timeline before we began; if we had made one, we would not have come close to meeting it. A faster process would have appeared more efficient, but it would have likely derailed other efforts, left teachers feeling unheard, and caused some significant errors.
>
> (Jones, 2018)

A second is to anticipate, allow for, and accommodate extended faculty deliberation and collaborative work. This is not a light lift for hard-working, already stretched teachers, and it will both demand and develop faculty collaboration skills (Jones, 2018).

A third is to draw upon best practices in curriculum design and those teachers who are already most proficient in these practices. At root, this is an exercise in backward design: conceptualizing intended outcomes before planning the tasks and learning in which students understand, practice, and demonstrate those competencies (Jones, 2018).

Spain, France, Italy, and China

School Year Abroad (SYA) offers year-long learning programs in four countries for US students; in addition to living with a family and immersing themselves in the culture, students attend regular school taught by a team of SYA teachers. Recently, it undertook a thorough process to reconsider its educational philosophy and approach, and ensure it was exploiting its unique educational opportunities. As one of its administrators, Aric Vissar, explained:

> How can we as an organization make sure we're taking advantage of the situation we're in? We're not trying to be good at what most schools are good at. We're trying to be something different. We have some advantages that other schools don't.
>
> (Hudson, 2018)

It was this that led SYA to recognize the value that competency-based education and assessment could provide. As Eric Hudson explains in a blog post, "its focus on immersive experiences, deep language learning, and intercultural competency makes it uniquely suited to competency-based learning, where skill development and exhibitions of learning take priority over seat time and traditional modes of assessment." In its second step in this process, SYA developed a set of program-specific competencies and engaged Hudson's team from Global Online Academy (GOA) to assist them. Before diving in, though, SYA educators immersed themselves in the language, the forms, the research, and available writings about CBE (Hudson, 2018).

This prepared them for the heart of the work: determining the competencies. Teachers worked in small groups, reflecting upon the program's distinctive qualities and aspirations, drafting language, using gallery walks by which drafts could be posted and commented upon, revising their work, and voting in a preliminary set of SYA core competencies—all in one day (Hudson, 2018).

The next several days addressed assessments, considering how to use those statements to inform the kind of learning and work students do and how to assess them appropriately. Reflecting on the progress, SYA administrator Vissar says:

> Our school with four campuses feels more unified today than it ever has. It's unified for all the right reasons: around a common set of values and goals for the best way for students to engage in the study abroad experience in a way that they wouldn't be able to do if we left things to chance.

(Hudson, 2018)

California: Central Valley

The transformation of the Lindsay Unified School district in California's Central Valley is recounted in a 2017 book entitled *Beyond Reform: Systemic Shifts Toward Personalized Learning*. The district serves mostly migrant farmer families, with more than 90% qualifying for free or reduced lunch, more than 90% Hispanic. Before its improvement work, it had only a 70% graduation rate and a 20% college enrollment rate (Lindsay Unified School District, 2017).

Their embrace of personalized learning entailed advancement only by mastery, not seat time. They began their work, in 2005, expecting that district leaders, board members, and administrators alike would be continuous learners themselves, committing to inquiry and study of the changing educational landscape. They engaged the community, bringing in 150 stakeholders for a two-day workshop that addressed five key questions—most notably, what should graduates know and be able to do? They changed the vocabulary of schooling to reflect and reinforce systemic change in expectations and norms: students became learners, teachers became facilitators, schools became learning communities (Lindsay Unified School District, 2017).

Most importantly, they adopted a mastery mindset throughout the district, in which "learners take as much or as little time as they need to learn the content and then move on when they are ready." Teachers (facilitators) must "skillfully integrate multiple opportunities for learners to demonstrate mastery into their lessons through the use of formative assessment, digital learning tools," and more. Seven socio-emotional competencies were identified as essential outcomes of a Lindsay education. Teams of teachers unpacked the California state standards, "identifying all learning as simple or complex knowledge, [and then] created progression of learning targets." For each learning target, they created a rubric "that clearly identifies the components of mastery" (Lindsay Unified School District, 2017).

With the system entirely in place, and student progression exclusively on the basis of standards mastered, the district did realize that there was a mismatch of the reporting they provided to students and what they needed to provide to colleges. Accordingly, a conversion table was established. The authors, the architects of the Lindsay transformation, offer several considerations for educators exploring or implementing similar transitions. One is to "involve learners from the beginning," valuing their voices and testing concepts regularly with students; another is to keep the "strategic design" prominent, front and center, in all the work of the system. "When embraced and lived out by all stakeholders, the vision gives people a higher level of purpose in their roles and becomes an intrinsic motivator." Also emphasized is adult learning, not just at the beginning of the process but throughout. A fourth key element is monitoring and continuous improvement: "site-based teams will plan, monitor, and adjust instruction to ensure" goals are met (Lindsay Unified School District, 2017).

Lessons for Leading Change

Readers are encouraged to review these seven case studies of school or system transformation and take the insights that are most pertinent to their circumstances and aspirations. There is no one-size-fits-all strategy that will suffice.

Seven themes stand out most significantly:

1. Constituency communications
2. More than buy-in, co-creation
3. Adult inquiry, learning, and research
4. Student learning and students at the center
5. Collaboration not isolation
6. Patience
7. Start somewhere, and build iteratively

Constituency Communications

Begin communicating early, and continue communicating often. Pursue many channels of communication, not just school newsletters, and promote two-way communications by regularly inviting and encouraging constituents to join educators in dialogue, especially around the goals, purposes, and concerns regarding the work.

More than Buy-In, Co-Creation

Yes, "buy-in" is essential, but recognize that the greatest success will come not from persuasion or some form of subtle, idealistic, or high-minded psychological manipulation, it will come from co-creation. Co-creation entails holding off on defining too much of the form to the new system before fully engaging educational colleagues, and perhaps even students, in a ground-up design of the program. It is about starting from the beginning with the educators who will be responsible for the implementation, beginning with setting goals and defining purposes, and then designing the form to fulfill the function.

Adult Inquiry, Learning, and Research

In many of the narratives above, the transformative design was inspired and deeply informed by educators who were curious, widely read, and strongly networked with other educators. This kind of transformation is extraordinarily complex, but fortunately, there is a lot of literature and there are many exemplars to engage with and learn from. Take the time to educate your community widely and deeply in what this all means and how it works before and as you proceed.

Student Learning and Students at the Center

Educators frequently parrot the sentiment that it's all about the students, but the expression sometimes becomes the substitute for the reality. At the startup of this work, firmly establish what are the needs and interests of students in this fast-changing world. Do so in a process that includes researching the changing nature of work and higher education, and do so with surveys or focus groups of young alumni and current students. Distill those needs and interests into a short but strong statement that can be regularly referred to. Consider as a planning team: Can students be team members? How often can we tap student voice, and engage students as co-creators and prototypers?

Collaboration Not Isolation

Whatever the size of your organization, don't do this work alone. Seek out co-conspirators widely from your network of collegial schools and districts. Co-create together, pilot and prototype independently, convene again to compare notes.

Patience

In examples from as large as the nation of New Zealand to as small as a single small independent school in Vermont, educators are reporting this to be as much as a ten-year or more process. Don't hurry it.

Start Somewhere, and Build Iteratively

On the other hand, don't not start. The work will take a long time, but it needs to begin soon. Pencil a game plan, invite folks in, and start building models that define goals and identify competencies. Do it today.

References

DeLorenzo, R. A. (2009). *Delivering On the Promise: The Education Revolution*. Bloomington, IN: Solution Tree.

Hudson, E. (2018, July 19). Preparing for Competency-Based Learning: GOA's Partnership with School Year Abroad. Retrieved September 17, 2018, from https://globalonlineacademy.org/insights/articles/preparing-for-competency-based-learning-goas-partnership-with-school-year-abroad

Jones, E. (2018). Another Take on Assessments as One School Creates a Portfolio-Based System. Retrieved September 17, 2018, from www.nais.org/magazine/independent-school/summer-2018/another-take-on-assessments-as-one-school-creates-a-portfolio-based-system/

Keesee, N. (2017). The Shift to Competency-Based Education. Retrieved September 17, 2018, from http://mastery.org/theshift/

Lindsay Unified School District (2017). *Beyond Reform: Systemic Shifts Toward Personalize Learning*. Bloomington, IN: Marzano Research.

Peller, M. (2018, June 10). On Nueva and the Mastery Transcript. Retrieved September 17, 2018, from https://medium.com/@mike.peller/on-nueva-and-the-mastery-transcript-96b63d77f0e0

Wells, R. (2016). *A Learner's Paradise: How New Zealand is Reimagining Education*. Irvine, CA: EdTechTeam Press.

7

Planning the Shift

A Game Plan

The previous chapter laid out seven key strategies for leading the change to competency-based crediting. Among them was to take the long view, be patient, and understand the process as entailing many steps over several years. As in all large and complex projects, the work is best tackled by breaking it down into small and sequenced chunks.

Proposed below is a many-stepped sequence for leading or supporting a school or district in making this significant shift. Remember, this is not a process to be hurried; it would likely be spread out over a period of two to four, or even perhaps ten or more years. These steps aren't rigid in form, content, or sequence; every organization undertaking this work will need to prepare its own sequenced plan adapted to its own particular dynamics.

I. Laying a Foundation

    1. Conceptualizing the Big Picture
    2. Forging an Inclusive Planning Team

II. Crafting an Inclusive Vision

    3. Engaging Constituencies and Collaborators Early
    4. Hosting Community Forums for Visioning
    5. Establishing Vision, Goals, and Plans

III. Preparing the Organization

    6. Establishing Policies, and Securing Permissions and Waivers
    7. Identifying and Planning for Obstacles
    8. Promoting Effective Communication

I. Laying a Foundation

1. Conceptualizing the Big Picture

The process begins with leadership taking a high-level view of purpose and goals. Every step of the way, leaders will be asked why: Why are we exploring this alternative, and why are we undertaking this expansive process? Leaders need to answer in ways concise, compelling, and convincing. These answers ought to be authentic: personal and pertinent to the local context. It won't do to parrot the thinking or language of others. If the leadership doesn't genuinely understand why this work is underway, nobody else will, either.

Preparing to address the reasons why requires a deep understanding of what the project entails and what a new transcript and competency-based crediting system will accomplish. Leaders will need to study the topic thoroughly and become proficient in and conversant about its content and complexity. Books and articles should be read; conferences and meetings attended.

Secure the support of the organization's governing body. A shift of this significance in most cases will require organizational governance-level policy changes. But even if the organization leaves this type of policy determination entirely to the administration, it would still be wise for leadership to have the informed backing of the board before proceeding. Ideally, this initial step of securing support for the process might happen quietly, without making a big public splash, with policy-level decision-making deferred to much later phases. Open-meeting laws, however, which vary state to state, must be considered as to whether behind-the-scenes preliminary conversations and agreements are appropriate and legal.

Leadership is also encouraged early to scan the environment and identify so-called "bright spots." As science fiction author William Gibson famously said, "the future is already here, it just isn't very evenly distributed" (Gibson, 1999). This probably is true for your organization. Are some or many teachers already using elements of competency-based teaching practice? Are departments or grade levels already identifying overarching competencies, and are they designing tasks and using rubrics to assess them?

These "bright spots" are key to change management (Heath & Heath, 2010). Spotlighting them can help provide vivid and concrete examples of the change you are seeking, and narrow the perceived distance from where you are beginning to where you are going. Highlighting them helps reassure constituents that the change won't be so scary, that the new reality won't be so different.

"Bright spot" educators can be allies and advocates, and can help demonstrate to the broader community that the shift you are undertaking isn't a "foreign" intervention but a continuation or extension of good practices already existing within your school. Further, understanding these "bright spots" and how they've been successful within your context will help you consider how to expand them.

Determine your goals. Is your goal to adopt and implement competency-based crediting as soon as possible? Or is it your intent to simply to explore competency-based educational practices for suitability in your school, to educate yourselves and your community on best practices for assessment and instruction, and to experiment with pilots before seeing what emerges? This will be an important decision for leadership to make rather early in the process.

2. Forging an Inclusive Planning Team

Step two is simple: form a steering/planning committee. This should be a representative group of administrators and teachers; some organizations may choose to include board members, parents, and perhaps even mature students. If there are members of your community who are widely respected for their educational expertise, they might also be included. The best steering committees are no larger than eight or ten persons: it may not be possible to be entirely representative.

In their book, *Breaking with Tradition*, authors Stack and Vander Els suggest the "guiding committee" include these four types: "smart leaders" from the faculty who are widely respected or influential; "data hounds" who are savvy with administrative systems and data collection and analysis; "public relations" masterminds who will help coordinate communications; and "go-getters" who are early adopters themselves and who will provide the necessary urgency to keep the process moving (Stack & Vander Els, 2017).

The steering committee should meet regularly, perhaps every three weeks or monthly, partially depending on the pace of change being undertaken. The committee will need strong leadership for agenda-setting and memorializing of decisions. It will also need some organizational support for meeting rooms, supplies, refreshments, and resources such as books and advisers.

II. Crafting an Inclusive Vision

3. Engaging Constituencies and Collaborators Early

Working with the steering committee, leadership should form early outreach to key constituencies, particularly teachers, parents, and students. In some cases, it might make sense to organize advisory committees for each constituency that meets quarterly or biannually. These groups should have some preliminary introduction to the process that leadership is launching, the role of the steering committee, and the intended goals, with a particular emphasis on student learning and preparation for success in a changing world of work and citizenship.

4. Hosting Community Forums for Visioning

Broad community engagement will contribute to the overall success of the work, and this is the best time to establish that. These activities can be seen as a type of charrette such as is used in architectural design or urban planning. As explained by one organization,

> A charrette is a type of participatory planning process that assembles an interdisciplinary team to create a design and implementation

plan for a specific project . . . A key component of the charrette is time compression. For four to seven days, participants work together in brainstorming sessions, sketching workshops, and other exercises through a series of feedback loops. Meetings take place with participants coming together as a group at set times or breaking off into smaller working groups. Behind the scenes, the core design team works constantly.

(Charrettes, n.d.)

For this process, establish one or more driving questions to guide the process. Possibilities might include:

- What is the purpose of learning at our school/in our district?
- What do we want our graduates to know and be prepared to do when they leave?
- What should it mean to be a learner in our organization?
- How do we want to align our reporting, crediting, assessment, and instructional practices to our answers to the previous questions?

Charrettes usually comprise carefully facilitated, widely inclusive, vigorous working sessions with representative groups. It is no small undertaking, but consider opening the events widely, perhaps hosting upwards of 100–200 persons from all areas of your educational community.

An opening event, or session, might include testimonials from recognized and respected teachers, students, alumni, and parents who share what's most important about learning, what's most lasting from that learning, and what the greatest impacts of their educational experiences have been. Undertake a careful process of review and reflection on the organizational mission, vision, values, and history. Use all this information to discuss and determine a statement of the purpose of learning.

In a second day or session, presentations might be made about the future of work and citizenship, about the changing world economy and changing lifestyles, using local or regional experts and online videos. Invite participants to reflect on the previous session, and review other sources and their own experiences to explore and draft a list of key overarching skills that graduates must master prior to "crossing the stage" on graduation day. Label these something like Essential Skills, Core Competencies, or Priority Institutional Impacts.

Author and educator Jay McTighe writes about the importance of making mission statements more concrete and action-oriented by stating "specifically the desired results in terms of student learning." He calls these results the "impacts," and explains that these desired student learning results or impacts are "long term in nature (they develop and deepen over time); are performance based (they involve application by the learner); involve transfer (application occurs in new situations); [and] call for autonomous performance from the learner" (McTighe & Curtis, 2016).

In a third session, invite teachers, students, parents, and alumni to reflect upon, discuss, and share what they like and dislike about assessment, grading, and crediting. Dig into issues of clarity and transparency, equity and effectiveness, substance and significance. How well aligned are these practices with the educational purposes, lasting impacts, and core competencies established in previous sessions? Facilitate a post-it session, identify themes, generate a compelling statement for what you hope grading and crediting can accomplish and how they will serve and reflect the previously determined vision of student learning.

In a fourth session, consider using a "future protocol" to work backward from an imagined future when the "vision" has been fully implemented. This protocol can be found online at the website of the National School Reform Faculty. In it, participants imagine themselves as already living in that future moment with the goals fulfilled, and first identify what it looks and feels like to be there. They then look "back" to the beginning of the change initiative, considering how different things were "before," and then most importantly, talk through and list the steps they took to get to where they are "now." In itemizing those steps, dig into what needed to happen, what were the hardest parts of the process, where things went awry and needed course correction, and what were the most critical transition moments. Document all this for building your change management plan (NSRF, 2014).

Note: Ideally all four charrette sessions described above will be held with full community participation in large community forums, but if necessary, some sessions, and particularly the fourth, could be conducted with the steering committee alone.

5. Establishing Vision, Goals, and Plans

By now, a great deal of learning has taken place about the changes being envisioned, and a great deal of data has been collected from all constituencies about their aspirations for student learning. Now is the time for the academic leadership, working with the steering committee, to draft, share, and publish a vision for the future. This vision should focus on student learning and successful preparation; it should draw heavily upon and make explicit connections to the organization's history, mission, and philosophy; it should reference and quote voices from the charrette process and honor that input; it should be idealistic and ambitious; and it should paint a picture of the student experience upon its fulfillment. A vision that doesn't motivate teachers and parents, that doesn't inspire and inform the future of learning, will fail to accomplish this critically important phase.

There are additional desired elements of the vision:

A. It should create a sense of urgency. Educators argue about the accuracy of the 1983 Reagan Administration report, *A Nation At Risk*. But no one can dispute that it used language effectively to move its audience. One quote is unforgettable: "If an unfriendly foreign power had attempted to impose on America the mediocre educational performance that exists today, we might well have viewed it as an act of war" (National Commission on Excellence in Education, 1983). Establishing this urgency is so essential that it is step one of Kotter's well-known model of change management. Scott Looney, the founder of the Mastery Transcript Consortium, demonstrates this sense of urgency in everything he writes and says, explaining with emotion that students are suffering, that the current system allows for "atrocities," and that our children need us to do something now.

B. It should clarify what will remain the same. In a 2018 Harvard Business Review article, the authors write:

> a root cause of resistance to change is that employees identify with and care for their organizations. People fear that after the change, the organization will no longer be the organization they value and identify with—and the higher the uncertainty surrounding the change, the more they anticipate such threats to the organizational identity they hold dear. Counterintuitively, then, effective change leadership has to emphasize continuity—how what is central to "who we are" as an organization will be preserved, despite the uncertainty and changes on the horizon.
>
> (Knippenberg, 2018)

Ensure that the vision underscores what will remain the same after the new transcript is implemented, especially elements people are most passionate about: excellent instruction; high standards; college and career readiness; athletics and extracurriculars; strong and caring relationships; reputation.

C. It should answer the question why. Every leader in this transformational process—every academic administrator, board member, and steering committee member—should have an "elevator speech" in which they can convey concisely and consistently the answer to the inevitable question: Why are we doing this? This elevator speech answer must align to and be well supported by the vision statement. As Simon Sinek says in his TED Talk, "People don't buy what you do; they buy why you do it. If you talk about what you believe, you will attract those who believe what you believe" (Sinek, 2009).

D. It should narrow the distance between the status quo and the new reality. Explain clearly the ways in which these practices are already happening or being supported; explain how this future state will build on the present and will be relatively easily executed. It is understandable the leadership might feel that the work is daunting and the change management extensive, but don't convey that in the vision.

In the 2019 book, *Demonstrating Student Mastery*, the author explains that some purposes work better than others when articulating your vision and goals for this kind of change. Personalizing instruction, fostering reflection, and improving understanding of mastery and standards all add value, but he cautions against purposes such as focusing on technology or "the state/district is making us do it." Regarding the latter he writes, "When the entire motivation for a school is based on compliance, any initiative will lose its power . . . When a school, and particularly its leadership, is simply going through the motions, teachers and students can tell and respond accordingly" (Niguidula, 2019).

The vision then must inform the development of a comprehensive strategic plan. That plan will need to address and answer—or plan clearly when and how to answer—many critical questions.

- Does the work underway represent a full-board commitment to a new transcript and crediting system, or is the work more exploratory and provisional, determining whether or not to adopt this alternative and testing its viability?

- Will the new transcript be implemented for all students—or will it exist as an alternate option for only some students to select, while the status quo remains alongside?
- Is the change to a new transcript intended to have broad and highly significant "downstream effects" on instruction, curriculum, and assessment? Or is it more a change on the margins, simply swapping out course credits for competency credits?

The answers to some of these questions will come from the vision, and the two documents will need to be aligned.

The plan will also need to provide a clear timeline and series of specific steps and benchmarks to establish progress along the path to the new system—though as clearly laid out as these should be in the plan, they should avoid rigidity and overcommitting to particular dates; almost inevitably there will need to be adjustments made throughout the journey. Resource allocations should be clarified as well. The financial needs for consultation, communication, and faculty professional learning may be significant. Time, too, is a resource needing allocation: How will time be made available for the steering committee, for the competency writing, for the teacher learning? Finally, the plan ought to seek to identify what policy changes will be required. What changes will need to be adopted by the board of directors? What approvals or filings will be needed from or for the district, the state board of education, and the accrediting agencies?

In *Breaking with Tradition*, the authors write:

> One of the biggest reasons a school is unsuccessful in a shift to competency-based learning happens at this critical strategic planning and vision step because the school or guiding team does not take the time to outline a clear vision and detailed strategy for that future reality, leaving too much to interpretation.
>
> (Stack & Vander Els, 2017)

III. Preparing the Organization

6. Establishing Policies, and Securing Permissions and Waivers

Some schools and districts may find this process takes several years, and perhaps insurmountable bureaucratic hurdles may arise. Policies and permissions will vary widely among districts, states, state universities, and accrediting agencies: there is no way to identify them all here. This task may need to be assigned to a senior administrator as a job responsibility of some substance for a year or two. It is recommended to not do this work alone: form alliances with other schools or districts in your state and/or accrediting region, and plan together what to communicate and how to support each other. Support and resources for this can be found from the Competency Works website, the New England Secondary School Consortium, and the Mastery Transcript Consortium.

7. Identifying and Planning for Obstacles

Scan your landscape: Where will the greatest obstacles emerge? Working with the steering committee, conduct surveys and focus groups, and identify what will be the greatest sources of opposition and most difficult challenges that will complicate progress. Might they be affluent parents, the local newspaper, veteran teachers, union rules, ornery board members? Is the problem more one of uninformed attitudes, instinctive opposition-taking, fear of change? Identify your opposition and obstacles, unpack what underlies them, and make a plan for addressing or resolving them. This might be a listening tour, an education campaign, a lobbying effort, or a mobilization of allies.

Stack and Vander Els identify three of the most common type of "blockers," and for each, a tactic to address that form of opposition. For the "overworked teacher," they suggest "continuing to hold them accountable to their team and to the work of the school" (Stack & Vander Els, 2017). Other tactics might include acknowledging that teachers will need time to make this transition, and making creative or courageous choices with the schedule to provide this time.

For the "concerned for their child's transcript blockers," they suggest leaders "develop trust and working relationships with them," and emphasize that colleges will receive "more enhanced information than they have historically" (Stack & Vander Els, 2017). Those tips might help, but much more will be necessary: Consider attaining supportive testimonials from the types of colleges their children attend, and collecting and distributing data that demonstrate that students are not disadvantaged.

For the "guinea-pig student blocker," they recommend ensuring students have "choice and voice in their learning" (Stack & Vander Els, 2017). Leaders might also include students on steering committees, regularly communicate with identified students respected as peer influencers, and show students successful models of the new system in practice, through videos and testimonials from students in those school settings.

8. Promoting Effective Communication

Plans for effective two-way communication with all key constituencies, and parents especially, will need to be prepared with great care and attention. Don't dismiss parental fears or opposition as unfounded or hysterical; this process will founder if these concerns aren't honored and effectively addressed with evidence and example.

In a 2017 online article, advice is offered on getting stakeholders on board when "ditching" traditional grades. In it, a Washington DC principal offered his perspective:

> Jeff Heyck-Williams, competency-based brother-in-arms and director of curriculum and instruction at Two Rivers Public Charter School in DC, has been getting parents comfortable with alternative grading for the last thirteen years. For him, there are no shortcuts to buy-in: it's all about transparent—and frequent—communication.
>
> "At Two Rivers, we don't believe grades really give parents a sense of how their children are doing," Heyck-Williams explains. "A B+ in math may hide the fact that while a student is good at graphing, he may be struggling with calculations." He says the trick to getting families on board is demonstrating that value of a different approach.
>
> Throughout the year, Two Rivers holds four student-led, parent-teacher conferences. Heyck-Williams says these conferences help families understand the grading system, as students sit down with the data to discuss their strengths and weaknesses. "Having students talk about their own goals is a really powerful way for parents to understand why this way of grading meaningful," he explains.
>
> (Curtis, 2018)

A caution: Communication can overwhelm as well as inform. Chunk out your messages and education; work to ensure your community can digest what you are explaining in an ongoing, step-by-step process. Stack and Vander Els recommend itemizing each of the elements of the new system, and creating a calendar by which each is shared, one month at a time (Stack & Vander Els, 2017).

Another key part of the communication plan is celebrating small victories along the way. The community needs to appreciate that progress is being made and the results are worth the effort, and so to keep them engaged, help them see and embrace each win that occurs along the way.

9. Providing Faculty Learning and Support

Your school or district's professional learning director, academic dean, or dean of faculty will need to take a leading role in this work, perhaps the most important role. This transformation will live or die on the engagement, deep understanding, and skill sets of the faculty, and no expense of time or money should be spared to ramp up teacher capacity.

A valuable approach to promoting this learning for educators is to practice what you preach, to walk the talk. Identify the competencies required for educators to manage this transformation, and support them by providing the support and resources they need to develop and demonstrate these competencies, crediting them as they do. What better way for them to internalize the process than to live it themselves, as learners? This is the approach being taken and advocated by the Global Online Academy (GOA).

In an article published on the GOA site, administrator Susan Fine explains that some are surprised by their choice to establish a set of teacher competencies, but for their team, it has been key to their work implementing competency-based learning (CBL).

> While implementing CBL, we decided to be similarly transparent about what our teachers need to know and be able to do to design and facilitate GOA courses. To articulate the teacher competencies, we leaned on seven years of observing and working closely with our teachers, research on effective professional learning, student work and experiences, and student surveys.
>
> (Fine, 2018)

Fine shares the competencies they determined as most important.

1. Design and give feedback that leads to learning.
2. Write course-specific competencies and outcomes that guide design and enable students to set learning goals.

3. Design course architecture that leads students to develop agency and autonomy through competency-based learning experiences.
4. Build, foster, and participate in an inclusive learning community.
5. Reflect on, review, and revise design and facilitation.

(Fine, 2018)

Fine's is a fine list, but each organization should perhaps take time to build their own list of necessary educator competencies. Some to consider for inclusion would be rubric design and development; assessment inter-rater reliability planning; performance task craftsmanship; motivating and supporting high-quality student work product; work product revision and curation; and assessment validation.

For each of its defined five competencies, Fine explains that the GOA team has carefully built "outcomes and responses to the prompt what does this look like?" For the first one, about feedback, she shares these:

Outcomes: the teacher can . . .

- Design a sustainable and varied approach to feedback.
- Provide actionable, outcomes-based formative feedback and the time to digest and apply it.
- Identify evidence for how students' application of feedback leads to measurable progress.
- Write narrative comments rooted in competencies and outcomes drawn from student work.

What this looks like . . .

- Students live in a competency-based teaching and learning approach, using the language of competencies and outcomes fluently and consistently.
- Students receive timely feedback and opportunities to digest and apply it.
- Students create outcomes-based and actionable feedback for peers, who can apply it to improve.
- Students track their competency growth over time and target competencies to strengthen.

(Fine, 2018)

Faculty learning should surely be a case of learning by doing. There's no great value in lectures about what competency-based crediting is, why it is important, or how it is done elsewhere. Instead the time should be dedicated to doing the work: determining, writing, and unpacking competencies; crafting, adapting, and applying rubrics; revamping unit and lesson design; rethinking instructional roles; and retooling time management in the competency-based classroom.

Much of this professional learning will be most productive when conducted inside a professional learning community (PLC) context. Stack and Vander Els offer helpful insight on how to do so. They write that:

> A majority of the behind-the-scenes work in a competency-based learning system is accomplished during collaborative team time . . . Teams must identify the competencies and anchor standards to assess in their units of study; build performance assessments that truly measure those competencies; run the performance assessments through a vetting process for quality assurance; review and assess student work together; and then revise and refine the assessment accordingly . . . . Highly functioning PLCs are imperative for this work to occur at high levels.
>
> (Stack & Vander Els, 2017)

10. Crafting Initial Competencies

Now build the key components of the system. The first major element is the competencies themselves. At this juncture, the faculty and academic leadership should work together to review, select, and compose a set of preliminary competencies that reflect their school's academic goals and priority learning outcomes, both academic and nonacademic (social-emotional). Readers are directed to Chapter 4 to read more about this work.

11. Designing Performance Tasks and Rubrics

For students to earn competencies, they ought to demonstrate high proficiency, ideally by performing tasks that entail transfer of learning to novel situations and meeting rigorous intellectual and personal standards in doing so. Concerns will be great about the rigor and vigor of learning in the new system; demanding tasks and rubrics should go far in building confidence.

One starting place is an inventory of rich and robust performance tasks already in the program. It is possible that educators in your system have already established an excellent set that can be revised and repurposed for the work of assessing competencies; doing so will also add value in diminishing the degree of change that teachers, parents, and students have to experience.

Consider an exercise of grade level team teachers drafting interdisciplinary tasks that can be used to assess multiple competencies near the conclusion of that grade level, what McTighe in his book Leading Modern Learning calls "cornerstone tasks." He defines them as "performance tasks that elicit demonstrations of knowledge and skills valued in the wider world beyond school" (McTighe & Curtis, 2016). They should have these elements:

- Are performance-based, calling for the application and transfer of learning
- Establish authentic contexts for performance
- Integrate transdisciplinary impacts (such as critical thinking, technology use, and teamwork) with disciplinary content.

(McTighe & Curtis, 2016)

Similarly, inventory current rubrics for essential skills at use in your school, conduct self and/or peer assessment of them using rubrics for rubrics, revise them accordingly, identify rubric gaps, and conduct a process of enhancing rubric design and usage, and promoting consistent and/or universal rubrics for core competencies.

See Chapter 4 for more information.

IV.   Prototyping

12. Launching Pilots and Prototypes

By this time, much of the content of the new system has been built, at least in preliminary versions. Now, put them in place with students—perhaps for a semester, perhaps for a year or even two. Do so in a low-stake, provisional manner that allows your community to develop comfort with the mechanics of the new system, and allows leadership to evaluate what's working and what needs improvement. Call this phase a prototype or pilot; help people understand that you see this as learning, and communicate that failures, flaws, and mis-steps are not defeats but instead improvement opportunities.

There are many prototype scenarios.

- In a K-12 or 6-12 school or district, implement a competency-based crediting system for some or all seventh and eighth grade students. If possible, run the test for two years, all-in, acclimating these students to what their high school experience may be hereafter. Regularly have high school teachers observe the system and meet with seventh and eighth grade teachers to discuss lessons learned.
- With some or all of high school students, begin awarding badges for defined competencies, and tabulate them on a transcript addendum. With student or parent permission, include these addendum transcripts along with the conventional ones in what is sent to colleges. Ask for feedback from the receiving colleges.
- Establish optional Pass-Fail courses designed around a set of competencies in parts of the ninth grade program, with credit awarded based on competencies earned.
- Create an opt-in "school within a school" within which all courses or all students are graded pass/fail with competency badging or crediting.

13. Rethinking Instruction and Schedule

In the period during which pilots and prototypes are tested, don't let the energy for innovation and programmatic alignment flag. Conduct professional learning about the different modes of instruction that this kind of crediting will support or benefit from. Study your school schedule, anticipating the full implementation of the new system, and determine how schedule changes might better support competency-based learning and crediting. Don't leave these things to chance, or assume that they'll just naturally happen in time.

14. Touching-Back with Parents and Students

The prototyping phase demands continuous communication with parents and students. Disgruntlement unheard or unattended to will fester and undermine the advance of the transformation. Seek it out, surface it, and engage with it honestly and courageously. Host regular open meetings; conduct frequent short surveys; perhaps even provide an anonymous complaint "box." Ensure these key constituencies feel they are being heard; communicate publicly the way adjustments are made in response to concerns. Neither easy nor fun, this step can make or break your successful transition.

15. Reviewing and Refining Prototypes

Prototyping is a process of iteration; throughout the time allotted, teachers, academic leaders, and the steering committee should be evaluating effectiveness and adapting accordingly. There should also be a formal study period toward the end of this phase. It should include public meetings that welcome wide input; it should study data about student engagement, teacher and parent satisfaction, competencies earned and awarded, and a myriad of other quantifiable items.

The steering committee, together with the academic leadership, mustn't be afraid to extend the pilot phase, or suggest dramatic rethinking of aspects of the program. It is more important to get it right than to get it done quickly.

The committee should publish a report of their findings and recommendations, supported by data and example; this should be an act of transparency and trust-building.

16. Validating Competencies and Assessments

The stakes are now rising. Whereas for the most part, prototyping this model will have had little serious impact on student records and future opportunities, the pivot to fuller implementation brings with it a concordant need to check and confirm the reliability and validity of assessments. Here is when a careful and thorough round of rubric inter-rater reliability work might take place. It is also when concurrent validity studies should take place; predictive validity work would also be advised if possible, but would probably be unavailable at this juncture. Chapter 4 provides more information of how to undertake this important work.

V.   Launch

17. Implementation

At a certain point, whether with all students or some, schools must go all-in and implement the system. This may be one year after the process described here begins, or it may be ten, but no matter the length of time it takes, the point is to make it real in order to accomplish the goals set.

A few considerations for this largest of all steps.

Publish your school's competencies prominently on the website, and seek to educate your wider community about them, their importance and value, and why and how they were determined. Rally your community around the idea of competencies, not just courses: message throughout your region something to the effect that "at our school, students graduate with the skills necessary for success, not just a transcript."

Develop and distribute a "master" set of rubrics for all credit-earning competencies, and engage in a continuous process of study and revision of rubrics. Publish rubrics on the web, and add commentary or annotation that assists the unfamiliar parent or community member to recognize and appreciate the rigor they hold students accountable to.

With student and parent permission, publish and promote high-quality student work for which competency credits have been awarded. This can be a website gallery, a glass case in the school entrance hallway, or a series of newspaper articles or advertisements. Ensure it is impressive work: draw from academic studies at the highest level, and wow your community with the reality that student learning is deeper than ever before.

Send out your most articulate students and teachers to the community to speak and present at every civic and service club, every chamber and professional association meeting, every civic and community board, about the virtues and mechanics of the new system, and the powerful effects it is having.

Seek internship opportunities for students, and make highly visible to students and parents the alignment of particular internships with specific competencies, and the pathways they need to follow to generate work product for assessment and awarding of credit.

Consider how to make a section (or the entirety) of the library or information/media center into a personalized learning space, guided by educators who help students select competencies to pursue independently, guide them in finding quality resources, and assist them in generating work products or in passing high-quality assessments that will earn them those competency credits.

Form teacher teams from multiple disciplines to create interdisciplinary courses, or transdisciplinary inquiries, aligned to meet the requirements of multiple competencies, and then to facilitate learning pathways and resources for students to learn and demonstrate their mastery to earn the associated credits.

18. Continuous Improvement

Alongside implementation, a deliberate and well-structured process of continuous improvement should be designed and deployed. Match and align each of the key goals set for the new transcript and crediting system to specific metrics, and begin collecting data for those metrics before the system is implemented, as baseline data, and then ongoing throughout the first several years of implementation.

Quarterly or biannually, the steering committee should review metrics data, and determine adjustment necessary to continue carrying progress toward goals.

Things to consider:

- If SAT or ACT scores decline,
- If percentage of students admitted to first or second choice colleges declines,
- If student engagement declines,
- If student attendance declines,
- If teacher workload increases,
- If teacher turnover increases,
- If student self-reported or externally assessed social and emotional skills don't improve, or
- If any of a number of other important school-designated outcomes decline,

then adjustments should be considered and implemented.

In the previously mentioned paper, *Measuring Mastery*, the authors recommend the preparation of external validation study. They called upon competency-based education leaders to:

> Continue to gather and report validity evidence for CBE assessments and performance standards, including comparisons of student outcomes against relevant comparison groups. For CBE programs to be viewed as an attractive alternative to traditional programs, students and employers need evidence that CBE graduates possess the same knowledge and skills as comparable traditional graduates and CBE graduates are equally successful after graduation.

> (McClarty & Gaertner, 2015)

References

Charettes (n.d.). Retrieved September 17, 2018, from https://urban-regeneration. worldbank.org/node/40

Curtis, J. (2018, March 13). Looking to Ditch Traditional Grades? Here's How to Get Stakeholders On Board. EdSurge. Retrieved September 17, 2018, from www.edsurge.com/news/2017-05-17-looking-to-ditch-traditional-grades-here-s-how-to-get-stakeholders-onboard

Fine, S. (2018, August 21). The Five Essential Skills Teachers Need to Lead Competency-Based Learning. Retrieved September 17, 2018, from https:// globalonlineacademy.org/insights/articles/the-five-essential-skills-teachers-need-to-lead-competency-based-learning

Gibson, William. (1999) The Science in Science Fiction. On Talk of the Nation, NPR (30 November 1999, Timecode 11:55).

Heath, C. & Heath, D. (2010). Switch: How to Change Things When Change is Hard. Toronto: Random House.

Knippenberg, M. (2018, August 15). Research: To Get People to Embrace Change, Emphasize What Will Stay the Same. Retrieved September 17, 2018, from https://hbr.org/2018/08/research-to-get-people-to-embrace-change-emphasize-what-will-stay-the-same

McClarty, K. & Gaertner, M. (2015). Measuring Mastery: Best Practices for Assessment in Competency-Based Education (Report). Washington, DC: Center on Higher Education Reform American Enterprise Institute.

McTighe, J. & Curtis, G. (2016). Leading Modern Learning: A Blueprint for Vision-Driven Schools. Bloomington, IN: Solution Tree.

National Commission on Excellence in Education. (1983). A Nation at Risk. Washington, DC: US Department of Education.

Niguidula, D. A. (2019). Demonstrating Student Mastery with Digital Badges and Portfolios. Alexandria, VA: ASCD.

NSRF (2014). NSRF Futures Protocol: Back to the Future. Retrieved September 17, 2018, from www.nsrfharmony.org/wp-content/uploads/2017/10/Futures-N_0.pdf

Sinek, S. (2009, September). How Great Leaders Inspire Action. (Video file). Retrieved September 17, 2018, from www.ted.com/talks/simon_sinek_how_great_leaders_inspire_action

Stack, B. & Vander Els, J. (2017). Breaking with Tradition: The Shift to Competency-Based Learning in Plcs. Bloomington, IN: Solution Tree.

8

Perspectives from Higher Education

Speak to any educator, parent, or student about competency-based crediting and transcripts, and you're likely to encounter a similar set of questions and concerns. Sometimes the concern is that this alternate approach won't effectively convey what students have learned, and sometimes it is about whether it might be too "touchy-feely" and diminish academic rigor in secondary schools. But the most common question asked, by a large margin, is entirely understandable: How will college admission offices process these new transcripts when selecting students?

The question of how colleges will receive, manage, and fairly evaluate a competency-based credit transcript is at this juncture simply too premature to answer in any complete way. The models are still being developed; the communications between secondary school leaders promoting this change and the colleges who will need to use the new model have only just begun. Most often, when speaking to college admission officers, one quickly realizes how hard it is for them to even speak to the topic because they still have so much to learn, and one realizes also that there is still too much that is uncertain about the specific contents of the new form.

However, these conversations have begun, and we can report and discuss preliminary perspectives from higher education admissions. Doing so reveals critical things to which every educator working on this transformation should be alert when implementing change. Every educator reading this book and working to change the high school transcript should make the effort to speak to higher education admission officers both to understand their concerns and to better inform them about the purpose and procedures of the new system.

College and university leaders are educators, too, and often express genuine enthusiasm about the concept of a new type of transcript. Scott Looney's presentations about the mastery transcript include a quote from Georgetown University President Jack DeGioia, "We would be pleased to work with your group on this" (Looney, 2016).

Leon Botstein, president of Bard College, spoke similarly: "This is an extremely positive development that provides more of the kind of information that colleges need to assess whether a student can do independent intellectual and creative work that a first-rate college demands" (Jaschik, 2017, May 15).

Robert Massa, senior vice president for enrollment and institutional planning at Drew University, stated:

> The mastery transcript is an innovative approach to assessing what is really important in a student's educational development: analytical thinking, creativity, communication, integrity. I am strongly in favor of using nonacademic character traits as one factor in a college's admission decision. The mastery transcript moves us in this direction.
>
> (Jaschik, 2017, May 15)

Massa added in an interview that what the MTC schools intend to accomplish is "noble. When looking at skills students need for success in school and life, it is clear that to have them measured in high school and on the transcript would be very valuable. I think colleges and universities will embrace that" (Massa, 2018).

Todd Rinehart, University of Denver's vice chancellor for enrollment management, says that "in terms of doing right by students, this makes perfect sense" (Rinehart, 2018). Kasey Urquidez, vice president, enrollment management and dean, undergraduate admissions for the University of Arizona, sees the possibility of a new type of high school transcript as being just another way in which the broader educational landscape is fast-changing.

> It is already clear that the way we do things will become much more fluid in the coming decade. As a university we are anticipating that self-designed curriculum, self-directed learning, and competency-based education will be a much larger part of a University of Arizona

experience. If we have to process a different kind of high school transcript, that will just be part of this wide-ranging change, and we will evolve as we need to.

(Urquidez, 2018)

However, after an initial and high-level appreciation for the concept, administrators express anxiety about and begin to qualify their endorsement. Massa tells of mentioning the MTC at a national college admission conference to a room of 800 colleagues, and hearing what sounded like a "collective sigh of concern" from the audience (Massa, 2018).

One message heard commonly from admission officers is a preference for a competency-based record to be provided in addition to, not instead of, the conventional course record transcript. Michael Reilly, executive director of the American Association of Collegiate Registrars and Admissions Officers, offers a representative take.

My initial read is that this would be a good set of information to augment a traditional transcript but, by itself, could harm students seeking to attend institutions that are mandated to evaluate admissions, at least in part, on completion of a core set of courses and the performance (grades) in those courses.

(Jaschik, 2017, May 10)

Massa agrees, at least for the near future: "I would see us needing to retain some form of traditional assessment to be enhanced considerably by the mastery transcript" (Massa, 2018). Urquidez, too, asks for a "hybrid approach," at least at first.

Also requested is an extended process of transition. Registrar Association Director Reilly says that "until these are common currency, students would be negatively impacted when they seek to transfer to more traditional institutions if that is the only document they present" (Jaschik, 2017, May 10).

Both reactions are entirely understandable; indeed, schools are looking at providing both transcript forms in an interim phase, and extending that phase for at least several years. But a dual transcript strategy goes only a short distance toward reaching the goals set out for the competency-based crediting transcript model and the benefits for students it promises. Benefits delayed might be, for many students, benefits denied.

Preliminary Concerns

Some preliminary concerns from the higher education world can be grouped into nine themes. For each, a comment is provided—but not in every case can the objection be rebutted. For some concerns, there simply are no easy answers, at least at this point. MTC founder Looney regularly reminds his audience that he is in this for the long haul by necessity, because there are no quick fixes for some of these challenges.

1. Will There Be Information About Academic Subject Proficiency?

This is perhaps the paramount concern: what will be reported about student academic subject proficiency? Harvard Admissions Dean Bill Fitzsimmons told the *Boston Globe* of his concern:

> Secondary school grading systems and transcripts give colleges an estimate of how much a student has achieved day-to-day in the classroom and a way to measure a student's readiness for college-level academic work. We hope that the proposed proficiency-based transcripts will provide such information as well.
>
> (Krech, 2017)

Many others agree. "Judging an applicant's performance in high school courses—especially those related to the major the applicant hopes to pursue—is useful in determining if the applicant can handle the rigor of a college-level program," said James Roche, associate provost for enrollment management at the University of Massachusetts Amherst" (Krech, 2017).

Massa explained further: "We have to have some way to place students in appropriate courses, and how can we if we don't know if they've passed honors Biology or taken Calculus?" (Massa, 2018). Another commentator from outside higher education wrote in a critical article, "What happened to Newton's laws of motion, the causes of the Civil War, the ability to write a grammatical sentence, and the trained capacity to solve equations with two unknowns?" (Finn, 2017).

Inadvertently, perhaps, the MTC itself has contributed to this confusion and concern. Both Massa and Rinehart conveyed their perception that the MTC approach didn't include among its credits any academic subject competencies, and it's not surprising they and others might have misunderstood this. Graphics displayed on the MTC website (as of September 2018), and often used in MTC presentations and in articles about the MTC, show a sample set of competencies, and an illustration of the new transcript, that fail to fully and adequately represent academic knowledge (A New Model, n.d.).

The credits featured most prominently, in the largest font, as "Featured Credits" are "Foster integrity, honesty, fairness, and respect; Lead through influence; Build trust, resolve conflicts, and provide support for others; Coordinate tasks, manage groups, and delegate responsibilities; Implement decisions and meet goals; Persistence." All of these are certainly valuable skills, and it is refreshing to envision them as being worthy of high school learning and crediting. But none of them align well to the conventional academic subject proficiency that colleges seek to confirm students have attained. Digging deeper into the fine print, one can find at least one example of the kind of academic subject knowledge colleges are looking for, under Digital and Quantitative Literacy, a credit for "Master and use higher level mathematics." But it is just the one, and it isn't easy to locate in that dense block of text (A New Model, n.d.).

It will be important, even essential, for schools to explicitly and emphatically display—in bold font, on the top of their list—competency credits that clearly correspond to the academic subject proficiencies that colleges demand. "Master and use higher level mathematics" may or may not be enough; it'd be better to define competencies for more specific mathematical skills involving the use of derivatives to solve complex and unstructured problems in Calculus and the interpretation of ideological influence in historiography. Higher education admission officers have to know whether students have attained certain competencies when evaluating them for enrollment into STEM (science, technology, engineering, and mathematics) majors, for instance. If well executed, a competency-based transcript should do a better job than the current form in establishing this kind of academic eligibility—admission officers can see so much more in looking at the particular competencies, the associated rigorous rubrics, and seeing samples of student work, than an A− or B+ could show—but only if the competencies represent these skills.

2. What About Where Specific Course Completion Is Required?

James Roche, associate provost for enrollment management at The University of Massachusetts Amherst, also worries about state education policy, and how it might hinder eligibility of competency-based crediting transcripts.

For instance, the Massachusetts Board of Higher Education requires applicants to the University of Massachusetts and the state universities to have taken four years of English and math, three years of science, and two years of foreign languages, as well as other courses.

(Krech, 2017)

Urquidez, at the University of Arizona, spoke similarly about the requirements her Board of Regents establish for admission, unsure how they'd be applied to an alternative transcript.

It is unknown, as of this writing, how this obstacle will be surmounted, but clearly it will need to be confronted as the movement for the alternative transcript progresses. It may be as easy as crafting and publishing an accessible analysis that demonstrates, with evidence, how the accumulation of a certain set of competency credits equates to the completion of an associated high school course. In this case, schools will likely require these sets of credit as minimum thresholds for graduation and college eligibility. Whether that work will be easily executed, and whether it will meet the demands of higher education boards such as in Massachusetts and Arizona, remains to be seen. Of course, other alternate approaches may become dominant in the future, after extensive conversation and negotiation among secondary and higher ed institutions.

3. How Can We Trust That These Aren't Just a Teacher's Subjective Opinions? How Do We Have Confidence in These Credits?

This concern has been most loudly expressed outside the higher ed community, but college admissions officers may be thinking about this, as well. In an article for *Education Next* entitled "Fancy Private Schools Want to Abandon High School Transcripts and Grades," Chester Finn, senior fellow at the Hoover Institution, wrote dismissively that:

A founding group of one hundred schools—dubbing itself the Mastery Transcript Consortium—has set out to eliminate the high-school transcript and the pupil grades that go onto it, seeking instead to press colleges (and presumably employers and graduate schools) to evaluate their applicants holistically, basing those judgments on subjective reviews of the skills and competencies that individual pupils are said to have acquired during high school.

(Finn, 2017)

Changing the status quo challenges expectations and requires considerable adjustment of perspective. Finn seems to believe that current transcript letter grades reflect an objective rating of student knowledge and skills, an objectivity that will be lost in a competency credit alternative. But that is an inherent misunderstanding of the conventional model. Letter grades are nothing but, in most cases, a teacher's averaging of student performance on quizzes and tests, and sometimes papers, projects, homework, and class participation. And how are those performances rated? By a teacher's subjective review, nearly always individually, nearly always without carefully developed and validated rubrics. Indeed, grading and assessment experts from Guskey to Marzano to Brookhart have decried the inaccuracy and poor evidence basis of the contemporary grading system. Drew University's Massa agrees: "Standardized assessment may be missing from these new transcripts, but it's not there currently: letter grades now are not standardized" (Massa, 2018).

Once established, the new system should be far less subjective. Competencies, and the rubrics for assessing them, will be systematically developed, tested, and validated. Teachers will work collaboratively to administer assessments and establish inter-rater reliability. Reviewers will have easy access to the standards that teachers use in rating student performance (through the provided rubrics) and will be able to go beyond a teacher's "subjective" rating by accessing sample student work and reviewing it independently.

Massa urges "standardization of how competencies are defined and how they are assessed in a way familiar to us or that we can become familiar with" in the new model (Massa, 2018). "Consistency" was the mantra from the University of Arizona's Urquidez. "We already struggle with wildly varying high school transcripts; inconsistencies in this new transcript will only make it harder for us to treat students fairly."

Finn's and others' inaccurate perspective should be combatted vigorously in the evolving design of the model and the communications around it. Yield no ground in messaging: this new approach will be more evidence-based, more objective, and less subjective than anything that currently exists.

4. Will the Threshold for Earning and Awarding Competency or Mastery Credits Be Set High Enough?

Rinehart explained in an interview that when considering applicants for STEM majors, it is of the utmost importance to distinguish between students who earned Cs in STEM coursework from those who earned As. But would the MTC transcript permit him to make that distinction when reviewing students' STEM-related credits (Rinehart, 2018)? Massa concurs: "We need more than whether you have the competency or you don't; we need to know at what level competency you have performed" (Massa, 2018).

Arezu K. Corella, University of Arizona's assistant vice president for enrollment management, was most worried about this issue after reading articles about the Mastery Transcript Consortium, but looked at it from a different perspective. Instead of focusing on how they can best select from among qualified students, she wondered about whether they will lack information on student readiness. "How will we know if they can be successful when they arrive here?" (Corella, 2018).

The answer to this question partially lies in the rubrics employed to determine and award credits. The rubrics must hold students to a standard of competency or mastery that indicates readiness for success in future studies in STEM, as in this example, or college coursework generally. Validating this competency, as discussed in Chapter 4, will be critical, and once done, should be reported on the school profile information sent to colleges along with transcripts. Going further, it may be that schools will need to both define and declare persuasively that these credits simply cannot be earned/awarded for what was previously C-quality work. Students presenting work product that is of only C level simply will not earn credits. They won't fail either; instead, supportively, they'll be extended more time and resources, and encouraged to return to submit work when it is ready for A or B level credit. But there will no longer be room in schooling for what used to be called a "gentleman's C." And that's probably a good thing: who would want a neurologist, mechanic, hairdresser or personal care attendant who earned only a C in any competency important to their work?

5. How Long Will It Take to Adapt and Become Effective in Reading These Alternative Transcripts?

Admissions officers express concern that this is not a simple switch for admissions readers. They will need to learn how to efficiently read and process the new transcript, and they will need to understand the nuances of an individual school's systems and norms in awarding credits. Rinehart says it will be "cumbersome." Currently, selective university admissions departments have built up years of experience in understanding the standards and rigor of each high school individually, particularly those that regularly send applicants their way, and they use that knowledge when evaluating students' eligibility. But Rinehart cautions that it could take several years to replicate that degree of insight for the new system, and asks for an extended transition to support that (Rinehart, 2018).

Arizona's Corella agrees.

> We already have training now for holistic review, with a lot of framing about what to look for in applications to determine readiness. But for this, we'll need a lot more information about what the competencies really mean, especially the noncognitive competencies.
>
> (Corella, 2018)

6. How Will These Be Quantified for Quick Sorting and Ranking, Both for Admission and for Merit Scholarship?

Selective universities, even the many who practice "holistic assessment," still often use quantifiable data to sort the enormous volume of applications for easier processing, and depend on GPA for that sorting. Typically, GPA is combined with SAT/ACT scores to do this sorting, though increasingly colleges are now test-optional, leaving them with only GPA for this sort. The quantitative sort does not itself usually represent final decision-making, but it is does ease the complicated process, and admissions officers express anxiety about how what may become a large volume of uneasily quantified transcripts will do to their system.

Corella says that at Arizona, they receive 35,000 applications, and asks, "How will we do this efficiently, without hiring 25 more people, if there is no quantification of success in schooling?" (Corella, 2018).

Rinehart says that admissions officers have regularly confronted changes in the past, such as the emergence of weighted GPAs, and will adapt to change in the future, one way or another, because they'll have to. He is confident they will figure out the right way to make good admission decisions, and, for the most part, will make the right decisions in the future at the same rate they do currently. However, he says, what may become more challenging is the determination of merit scholarship awards, which, in his explanation, is even more dependent on GPA data than admission itself (Rinehart, 2018).

7. Will This Result in an Increased Emphasis on Standardized Testing?

Massa, Urquidez, and Rinehart have speculated that standardized testing results may become more important in admission selection when evaluating students with alternative transcripts. Many colleges have been working to diminish emphasis on standardized tests, due to the perception that test scores are too heavily influenced by socio-economic status or too limited in their prediction of college success. But when facing an unfamiliar transcript format, and lacking a GPA for quick assessment of academic preparation, many heavily burdened admissions departments might lean more on test scores than they would otherwise, and this may be an unintended and undesired outcome of the new model.

There is no easy solution to this concern. Might there be a way to quantify a mastery or competency transcript's data into a single, GPA-like score? If there were, would that compromise the goals and purpose of the new transcript? Might an extended transition, and extensive training for admissions officers, offset these concerns?

8. Will Students from Competency-Based Crediting High Schools Have a Difficult Transition to Traditionally Structured College Education?

This is a topic that often arises in conversations about progressive education, project-based learning, and alternative educational models. Those approaches, the logic goes, might be best for student learning, more evidence-based, more holistic and humane, and more supportive of learning for learning's sake. But colleges with traditional models that are expected to remain the same may worry that incoming students simply won't be able to adapt and thrive in their environments and advise to conform to be better prepared.

Urquidez believes that a new transcript form will change "everything." "This has implications for the whole education system. We'll need to really overhaul all of teaching and learning. Are the high schools looking at this new transcript prepared for all the changes in their practices this will require?" She asked that this "be a joint effort. Involve higher education early on in a genuine partnership" (Urquidez, 2018).

Drew's Massa expressed sincere concern about this, and has called for a united front.

> We have to be in this conversation together: secondary school educators along with higher ed admissions and also academic

deans to examine how best to ensure student success coming from competency-based environments to more traditional ones—and also to consider how higher ed itself might learn from and move toward the new model, because it has implications for how we teach at every level.

(Massa, 2018)

Massa added that "this is not a reason not to do this! We just have to find a way to ease into this."

9. Will This Crediting Model, and the Instructional Design That Leads to These Credits, Be Harder to Deliver in Poorly Funded Schools—and How Will That Influence Efforts Toward More Equitable Admission?

In Chapter 3, concerns of this kind about the mastery transcript were discussed, particularly as voiced by Catherine Rampell of the *Washington Post*. It is an issue much on the mind of Rinehart. In his view, it very well might enhance student learning and preparation, but likely will be much more easily supported in well-funded schools and by teachers with smaller student loads. Will that exacerbate the current inequity of college access?

Urquidez worried that the complexity of this system, and the ways in which it will be administered, "could cut against equity and access" (Urquidez, 2018). At the same time, her associate Corella saw a potential opportunity for low-income and first-generation secondary school students. Why couldn't a new transcript model provide students with credits for and meaningful recognition of the skills they develop and demonstrate by working jobs after school, or caring for younger siblings or older relatives in their home (Corella, 2018)?

Competency-based crediting advocates and planners need to consider carefully how the model can be made efficient and easily adopted across the diversity of school types in the US and globally.

References

A New Model (n.d.). Mastery Transcript Consortium. Retrieved September 17, 2018, from http://mastery.org/a-new-model/

Corella A. (2018, September 19). Personal Interview.

Finn, C. (2017, May 22). Fancy Private Schools Want to Abandon High School Transcripts and Grades. Retrieved September 17, 2018, from www.education-next.org/fancy-private-schools-want-abandon-high-school-transcripts-grades/

Jaschik, S. (2017, May 15). Experts Offer Range of Views on Plan to Kill High School Transcripts and Reform College Admissions. *Inside Higher Ed*. Retrieved September 17, 2018, from www.insidehighered.com/admissions/article/2017/05/15/experts-offer-range-views-plan-kill-high-school-transcripts-and-reform

Jaschik, S. (2017, May 10). Top Private High Schools Start Campaign to Kill Traditional Transcripts and Change College Admissions. Retrieved September 17, 2018, from www.insidehighered.com/news/2017/05/10/top-private-high-schools-start-campaign-kill-traditional-transcripts-and-change

Krech, A. (2017, July 9). What if Your High School Transcript Didn't Include Grades? *Boston Globe*. Retrieved September 17, 2018, from www.bostonglobe.com/metro/2017/07/09/what-your-high-school-transcript-didn-include-grades/h9V1ZtSTWQqWmqIBzbYwPJ/story.html

Looney, S. (2016, April 28). Mastery Transcript Consortium. Presentation given at Mastery Transcript Consortium Meeting in Cleveland Botanical Garden, Cleveland, Ohio.

Massa, R. (2018, September 4). Telephone interview.

Rinehart, T. (2018, September 14). Telephone interview.

Urquidez, K. (2018, September 19). Personal Interview.

9

Conclusion

Whether you have yet to start, have only just begun, or have already made considerable advances in this journey, the road ahead will be neither short nor simple. As you have read, there are some steep obstacles and swampy grounds. Almost inevitably, some who set out will fail to reach their intended destination. Others may, however, succeed gloriously in forever changing teaching and learning for the better.

But if and as you proceed, the following are some final thoughts for you to consider here, in closing.

1. The journey will be valuable for its own sake, regardless of whether or when you arrive at the destination. For your community to develop a greater proficiency in competency-based education, to determine what your school values most as key outcomes in student skills and knowledge, to design and practice quality rubrics to effectively assess these key skills, and to craft engaging and demanding performance tasks for students: all this will strengthen student learning for years or decades to come, even if your school never adopts a new transcript format. Think of this as a project-based learning exercise, where it is the educators who are inquiring, empathizing, researching, prototyping, iterating, and producing meaningful new educational programs and techniques.

2. Maintain a close focus on student learning and well-being. Remind yourself, and remind everyone else, that this hard work is for a higher-quality student learning experience. The current model isn't working. Students are suffering from competition, stress, and grade-grubbing in a compliance culture that diminishes intrinsic motivation and ultimately deprives them of the deeper learning and

skill mastery they most need. Everyone wants students to develop the powerful competencies most important for future success.

3. Promote and provide a more holistic education. Academic subject knowledge is necessary but not sufficient for student success today or tomorrow. Ensure that competencies include social and emotional skills such as persistence, resilience, self-management, collaboration, and problem-solving.

4. Go further with others; don't try to do this alone. This is complicated work that will daunt even the most informed and energetic leaders, and it depends on the collaboration and support of many external actors including higher education, state policymakers, and accrediting associations. Form associations with other schools in your region and state, and participate vigorously in your network's collaborative efforts and actions.

5. Maintain and elevate rigor and expectations. There will be a steady stream of negative messaging to the effect that this transition might lower academic standards or pamper students. Students don't need fewer skills or lesser proficiency in this day and age; they deserve better preparation than ever before, and we know that we can serve that purpose by holding the highest of expectations while providing them meaningful, rigorous, and engaging tasks: work that matters. Hold competency thresholds high; demand performance and transfer that goes far beyond the recapitulation exercises that mark so much of our contemporary secondary schooling.

6. Include every voice that matters in your process; no other educational change effort that you will ever participate in will demand so much, or benefit so greatly from a genuinely and thoroughly inclusive process. Host open forums, seek out anxious or disgruntled stakeholders, and demonstrate vividly how the process is honoring multiple perspectives.

7. Don't stop thinking about instruction. Defining, assessing, and recording competency credits may seem like the most important part of this work. But be wary of the example of New Zealand, which saw the intended implications of its transformative transcript corralled, in many cases, back into traditional molds of instruction. From early on and throughout the process, maintain attention to the way teaching can and should evolve to better serve the new system of crediting and, more importantly, the greater goal of positively transforming learning for all students.